DIY FASHIONISTA

THIS IS A CARLTON BOOK

Text copyright © Geneva Vanderzeil 2012
Special photography copyright © Geneva Vanderzeil and Ben McCarthy 2012
Design copyright © Carlton Books Limited 2012

This edition published in 2012 by
Carlton Books Limited
20 Mortimer Street
London W1T 3JW

10 9 8 7 6 5 4 3 2

A CIP catalogue record for this book is available from the British Library.

ISBN 978 1 78097 170 4

Printed and bound in Dubai

Senior Executive Editor: Lisa Dyer
Managing Art Director: Lucy Coley
Design: A&E Creative
Copy Editors: Jane Donovan and Nicky Gyopari
Production: Maria Petalidou

Key to Skill Levels

✂ **Easy project with no sewing**

✂ ✂ **More involved project with no sewing**

✂ ✂ ✂ **Simple hand-sewing project**

✂ ✂ ✂ ✂ **Simple machine-sewing project**

✂ ✂ ✂ ✂ ✂ **Machine-sewing project and simple pattern-making**

DIY FASHIONISTA

40 stylish projects to re-invent
and update your wardrobe

Geneva Vanderzeil

CARLTON
BOOKS

CONTENTS

INTRODUCTION

Like many women I have always dreamed of having the perfect wardrobe. A beautifully curated collection of basic and statement pieces that come together to offer countless outfit options. But that ideal has always been well out of reach, as my aspirations have often been far greater than my bank balance. Early on I learnt that by using simple sewing, embellishing, dyeing and reworking skills I could have the effortlessly stylish wardrobe I wanted without sacrificing my budget – and so my DIY obsession was born.

In this book I'll show you how to unleash your inner DIY fashionista, so that you too can have a perfect wardrobe made up of items you've created yourself. From the fundamentals of DIY fashion to how to get started on before-and-after reworking projects, I'll give you a step-by-step plan for revitalizing your current wardrobe, and teach you how to get the most out of your visits to thrift stores and secondhand shops. There are 40 classic and chic projects on the following pages, which can be reinterpreted a thousand different ways depending on the materials and skills you have to hand. Use this book as an inspirational journal, tag it, write in it and annotate it with your ideas. Save your notes between the pages and use the images as a reference when creating your own projects – because the DIY fashionista is always brainstorming how she'll create her next stylish outfit for the season ahead, for a steal.

The DIY Fashionista

I've always been addicted to fashion and clothes – one of my earliest memories is of my parents putting a lock on my wardrobe to stop me changing outfits every hour! Almost as soon as I could walk, my mother introduced me to shopping at secondhand stores and also instructed me on the basics of sewing. This was the start of a lifelong obsession with creating my own catwalk-inspired pieces.

My parents always emphasized the importance of thinking about the environment when making choices about what I wore, ate and did. As a young girl I was the only person I knew who had light switches which had little stickers on them saying, "Remember to turn off the light!". From a young age I used to buy clothes and accessories from my local secondhand store and alter them using my mother's hundred-year-old Singer sewing machine. I soon began reworking and redesigning vintage pieces I had picked up from markets and thrift stores, and this has grown into making accessories, shoes and even designing clothes from scratch. A love of fashion, a tiny budget and an awareness of the importance of "making do" created a solid foundation for my do-it-yourself fashion. Nowadays everything I see, whether it is in a magazine, on a website, on the street or in a store, I think, "Can I make that?". In 2010 I founded A Pair & A Spare, a website where I could share my inspiration and DIY projects with an audience from all around the world. From day one I set out to prove that DIY fashion can integrate with a glamorous and stylish wardrobe, and that you don't need to spend lots of money to have on-trend looks.

Why Buy When You Can DIY?

- **Perfect your wardrobe:** Create the wardrobe you've always wanted using secondhand clothes and inexpensive materials, many of which you may already have to hand.
- **Reinvent your style:** Rock the latest trends and constantly reinvent your style to keep in tune with the fashion seasons without breaking the bank.
- **Recycle and re-use:** Look stylish while being conscious of your consumption by making the most of your own closet or secondhand pieces.
- **Be empowered by your own creativity:** Have pride in your style and enjoy the satisfaction of knowing that what you're wearing you made with your own two hands.
- **Be yourself:** Put a spin on a look and make it unique by embellishing, reworking and redesigning.
- **Beat the high street:** Channel new season looks before they hit the high street using DIY.

Good Luck with your DIY projects!

HOW TO DIY IN 4 SIMPLE STEPS

1. Find inspiration

2. Collect materials

3. Gather essential tools

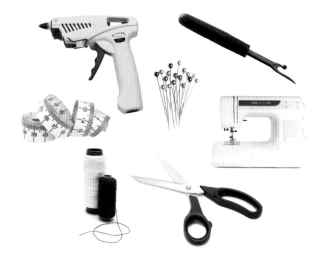

4. Make time

Are you a budding fashion DIY enthusiast at heart but don't know where to start when it comes to embarking on your first project? These four simple steps will get you started so that you too can have a customized self-made wardrobe, and be proud to wear pieces you've created by hand.

1. FIND INSPIRATION

Look around you for inspiration for DIY projects – in magazines, on blogs, fashion websites, on the streets, in shops or in your local department store. Once you start looking you will realize that almost every fashion item you see has an element that you can re-create yourself, given the time and materials. See pages 10–15 to read more about how to find, collect and organize your inspiration. DIY ideas can be fleeting, so holding onto them is essential.

2. COLLECT MATERIALS

Get together a collection of secondhand or outdated clothing, fabric remnants and cheap materials, such as chains, buttons, studs, ribbons and zips, which can be used to embellish items of clothing or accessories.

3. GATHER ESSENTIAL TOOLS

Organize a DIY essentials kit. This kit will have the key tools to support the actual process of your projects, and without them it's going to be difficult to follow through when you're inspired. There is a huge benefit in taking the time to collect the right basic tools at the beginning – it opens up your imagination and means there will be less barriers to getting started on a project. To do this, get a box and started collecting. At a minimum your essentials toolkit should contain the following:

• Dressmaker's scissors
• Dressmaker's pins
• Measuring tape
• Tailor's chalk
• Black and white thread
• Needles
• Seam ripper
• Assorted adhesives, including a hot glue gun.

If you can afford it, invest in a sewing machine. They are the best purchase you will ever make in terms of your ability to create high-quality and professional-looking projects. Share the investment with friends or seek out a sewing school to practice your skills prior to making the purchase.

4. MAKE TIME

Most of us lead busy lives and time is one of the biggest factors in being able to carry out DIY projects, but multitasking can be a great help. Why not do some DIY projects while watching television or on the commute to work – beading and other handsewing projects are possible. Still torn between other commitments? Organize to do projects with friends at "crafternoons" or DIY parties so that you can socialize while creating your perfect wardrobe.

INSPIRATION & MATERIALS

Finding inspiration and gathering materials for your projects are two of the first steps to embarking on DIY fashion projects. In this section I will talk you through how and where to look for these fundamentals.

Once you get a chance to make your DIY inspiration a reality and have chosen your project and materials, consider how the piece will integrate with your wardrobe and contribute to a range of different outfits. Choose to make projects that will be versatile among your existing ensembles so that you don't end up with a wardrobe full of mismatched handmade items that you never wear. In this book there are 40 classic projects that will integrate well with your wardrobe and are also able to be reinterpreted in different colours, materials and patterns.

FINDING INSPIRATION

Keeping a sharp eye out for inspiration will help you to create the chic and on-trend wardrobe you have always wanted without breaking the bank. Look around you – in magazines, websites, on the streets, in shops or in your local department store. Start asking yourself, "Could I DIY that?". As soon as you adopt a more critical eye when it comes to the things you buy, you will begin to realize that much of what you see can be made by hand, as long as you have the time, tools and right materials.

Collect inspiring images and ideas from websites, tear-sheets from magazines, and pictures taken of looks you see on the streets and store them in a box or a folder or in a file on your computer titled "DIYs to Do". DIY ideas can be fleeting, so make sure to capture your inspiration when you have it. This allows you to come back to it at a later time. Pictures of some of the items that have inspired me are shown on page 10.

SOURCING MATERIALS

Another key factor in the production of high-quality projects is the inventive use of a wide range of materials. Start collecting such materials as chains, buttons, beads, studs, ribbons and zips, which can be used to embellish items of clothing or accessories. Often you will find these in the most unlikely of places: thrift stores, hardware and plumbing stores, newsagents and stationary shops, and junkyards.

Stockpile items when you see them, even if you don't have a use for them at that particular moment – they always come in handy down the track. And when in doubt, always buy slightly more than you think you will need – there is nothing worse than starting a project and running out of a particular material mid-way through. I also usually try not to spend too much money on my materials; DIY is a way to satisfy your fashion cravings without breaking the bank.

Secondhand Clothing

The most simple DIYs involve altering and updating thrifted clothes – doing these sort of projects is what got me addicted to DIY in the first place! Creating a garment from scratch can be a daunting task, but making changes and alterations to existing clothes is a surprisingly easy place to start. Secondhand clothes are ideal, because the less you spend on these items, the more encouraged you are to be imaginative. Add fringing, studs, feathers and buttons as a start. Check out your local charity shops, consignment stores, flea markets and garage or car-boot sales for clothes to experiment on. In this book you'll find a guide to getting the most out of secondhand stores on page 15, and tips for reworking secondhand clothes in the Before & After section on pages 22–51.

Fabrics

A local craft or department store will most likely be your first port of call, however secondhand shops, which often have baskets of offcuts or rolls of wool, are likely to have the best-value fabrics. Find out if there are any fabric consignment shops local to you where you can pick up bolts of fabric or swatches that designers have discarded, or try ethnic markets and stalls for unique fabrics.

Haberdashery

One of the best places to source items such as thread, needles, zips and buttons is online on websites such as eBay. Make sure to check back regularly on auction sites as pieces become available all the time. You can often stock your whole kit for a steal.

Hardware Items

Surprisingly, hardware stores can be a treasure trove of potential materials if you apply some imagination. Visit your local store and try to imagine how you could use different items such as bronze piping (a necklace?), bright pink surveyor's tape (a bracelet?) or plastic sheeting (a chic transparent rain cape?). When it comes to the merchandise on sale in a hardware store, you are limited only in terms of your own imagination!

Jewellery and Beads

Keep your eyes peeled at flea markets, yard sales and in secondhand shops for broken jewellery, beads, jewellery findings and other items that can be used to make new statement pieces. It is always possible to fix and revitalize broken items and these sorts of pieces can be used to re-create something chic and on-trend.

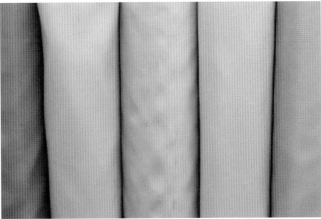

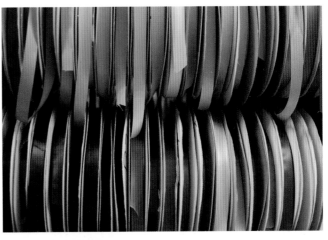

THRIFT SHOPPING: A 5-POINT PLAN TO GET THE MOST OUT OF SECONDHAND SHOPS

Secondhand or outdated clothes are the backbone of the best DIY projects, as they are a great way to experiment with ideas and techniques, plus most of us simply don't have the money to buy new. Here is some advice for finding the basic ingredients that you can then spend time embellishing, cutting, sewing or ripping to make something new and unique.

1. Go Often
Frequency is one of the most important factors when it comes to shopping in secondhand stores, as almost everything you find is going to be a one-off and if you don't scoop the great stuff someone else is going to. Things are coming and going all the time, so when you've found a great shop, go as often as possible.

2. Dig Deep
Don't be afraid to get your hands dirty and dig around: the best finds are often at the bottom of the pile. One treasure trove of goodies is the men's area – you can often pick up great silk shirts or trousers here. Often the volunteers don't know a pair of women's harem pants from a pair of men's trackie bottoms, so make sure to look high and low.

3. Be Imaginative
Use your imagination in terms of how certain items of clothing could be worn: try on silky tops and imagine them paired with skinny jeans and sky-high heels; think about wearing bulky patterned cardigans with leggings and flat boots; throw on a stripy 1980s swimsuit and consider wearing it with denim cut-offs. Also think outside the box in terms of categories – tops for bottoms, outerwear made into daywear, evening to day and so on. The options are limitless – you just need to create them in your mind.

4. Location, Location, Location!
Consider the location of the thrift shops you visit – particularly the catchment area and the demographics of the people who live there. The best jumbles are often found in places where a proportion of the population have a reasonable income, and it's here that you will be more likely to find better quality cast-offs. Thrift shops that have a high elderly population are usually great sources of amazing vintage clothes.

Charity shop depots or sorting stations with attached stores are other fantastic resources, as they act as a channel for a bigger catchment area and thus increase your chances. These are often located on the outskirts of cities and towns. Although they may be difficult to get to, they are definitely worth it.

5. Get to Know the Staff
Because the staff at secondhand stores are usually volunteering or working for next to nothing, it is worth being especially kind and helpful. Even better, become friends with the old lady who works at your local charity store and you might even find she puts things away from you.

SKILLS & TOOLS

The world of the DIY fashionista is one without limits, where any project is possible. Once you start looking at trends, styles and looks with a critical mind, you'll realize that, with the right foundations such as key skills and tools, you can re-create just about any style you see on the catwalk or in a magazine. Have the confidence to make your DIY ideas reality. Even successful crafters have a project graveyard, a place for those projects that didn't work out as planned. But remember, projects that go awry can always be refashioned in the future, so there is no such thing as a complete fail – if you use cheap and thrifted materials, you won't feel bad if they go wrong.

To me, DIY fashion is most successful when people around you can't tell you made it yourself – as this is the sign of a truly well-executed project. So choose your project with your own skills, and the ability to execute the project well, in mind. Start with simple projects, moving on to more complicated ones as you build your confidence and your skills. A few basics to get you started are on the following pages.

ADHESIVES

Adhesives have a key role in any DIY fashionista's toolkit, and certain formulas will be appropriate for specific projects, depending on your material and the strength of the bond required. The last thing you want is for your adhesives to fail and your item to fall apart. Read on to learn about the most common types and when they should be used.

HOT GLUE
The glue comes in stick form and must be heated up using a glue gun. The gun and glue will be very hot once heated and should be used carefully. This option is best for temporary projects and those that require low- to medium-strength bonds.

CRAFT/PVA GLUE
Available in a white liquid form, this glue dries clear. It is ideal for light-duty projects using porous materials like wood, paper, plastic and cloth.

ADHESIVE SPRAY
This spraycan adhesive disperses droplets of glue to form light coats. It is best for lightweight materials like plastics, photos, fabrics, paper, glitter and small pieces of wood and metal.

SUPERGLUE
Most often available in a tube (such as E6000 adhesive), these provide a strong and durable bond. Best for wood, rubber, glass, metal, ceramic, rope and jewellery.

FABRIC GLUE
Similar to PVA glue but often more flexible and washable, this is best used to secure embellishments such as rope, sequins and trimmings. It is not recommended in place of sewing for bonding garments together. Fusible webbing can be used to create simple hems with lightweight resistance.

SEWING SKILLS

Sewing is an incredibly useful skill for anyone interested in creating professional-looking results. Although some people shy away from sewing, thinking it may be too difficult or time consuming, it is very easy once you know the basics. This section will outline the broad skills you need to get started on the DIY projects contained in this book, looking firstly at hand-sewing and then machine-sewing.

Hand Sewing
Hand sewing allows you to make minor alterations to the shape and fit of a garment, mend any holes or tears, attach decoration and beading, and is often easier than machine-stitching on small projects and accessories. In the absence of a sewing machine, hand-sewing can also be used to undertake more time intensive projects too. I have hand-stitched a maxi skirt (see pages 62–5) before, and although it took a little longer than it would have on a machine it looked just as good. There are a few key techniques you will need to master hand-sewing.

HOW TO THREAD A NEEDLE
You need: A needle, thread and scissors.
1. Cut the length of thread you require.
2. Trim the end of the thread so it is a clean cut without fibres that may hinder the thread going through the eye of the needle.
3. Pass the freshly cut end through the eye of the needle. It's easier if you slightly dampen the end of the thread first.
4. For a normal stitch pull the thread two or three inches down and hold the end while sewing. For a stronger stitch pull the thread through the needle halfway and then double over the thread.

BASIC STITCHES
The stitches on the facing page are the basic ones you will regularly use when hand-sewing.

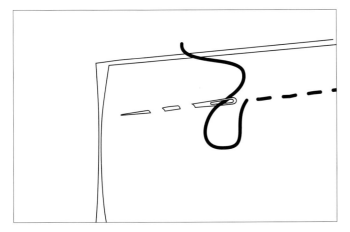

RUNNING STITCH

Perhaps the simplest of stitches, the thread runs straight through the fabric without doubling back on itself. Used to join fabric for gathering and mending.

WHIP STITCH

A basic stitch that is invisible when worked on the underside of the fabric, it can be used to form a hem or seam.

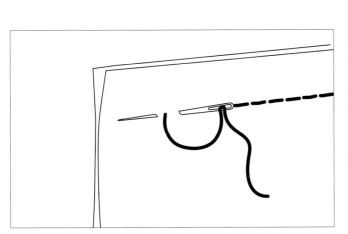

BACKSTITCH

A strong stitch, the backstitch is formed by pulling the needle through the fabric, then doubling it back on itself. The needle emerges beyond the stitch just made, and doubles back again for the next stitch. This is close to the type of stitch a machine does.

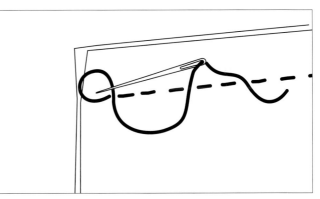

SECURING STITCH

This is done at the start and finish of your sewing to stop the stitches from coming undone.

1. Take one small backstitch and make a loop over the point of the needle.
2. Pull the thread through the loop to create a knot at the base of the fabric.
3. For a stronger secure stitch, repeat the process to create two knots.

Machine Sewing

Knowing the basics of machine sewing has changed my life in that it has allowed me to experiment with DIY projects that I never would have even thought about attempting by hand. A machine also makes it that much easier to finish projects quickly and efficiently.

CHOOSING A MACHINE

Buying a sewing machine can be a daunting task, particularly if you've never sewed before. Choose a basic machine that functions well, as you don't need a highly complicated machine to do any of the projects in this book, or indeed most basic projects. If you prefer, buy a secondhand machine – look for a used one in your local classified ads or online – or ask a friend or family member if they would loan or give you a machine they may no longer use.

MACHINE NEEDLES

There are various types of sewing needles available based on the type of stitch and fabric you are using. Needles come in different sizes appropriate to the thickness of the fabrics you are sewing and also with differently shaped points. Generally, it is best to keep three different sizes of universal needles on hand, which are midway between a point and a ball point and can be used on a wide variety of fabrics, the thinnest of which is for silks and thickest of which is for denims.

BASIC STITCHES

Although many machines have a huge number of stitches, the likelihood is that you will use only a limited number for your average sewing projects. Here are a few of the stitches I use most frequently.

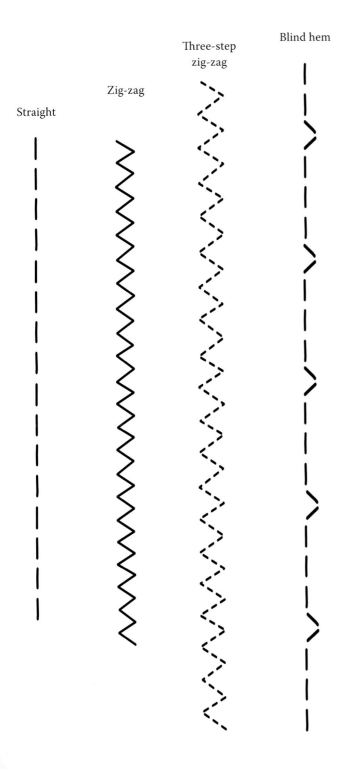

Straight

Zig-zag

Three-step
zig-zag

Blind hem

Straight: This is the stitch that you will use most often on your average DIY projects. You can use the straight stitch to sew seams, darts and hems.

Zig-zag: The zig-zag stitch can be used on stretch or knitted fabrics as it allows the seam to retain some flexibility.

Three-step zig-zag: The needle takes three stitches to one side and then three stitches to the other side. The three-step zig-zag is good for finishing raw edges in place of a selvedge overlocker.

Blind hem: This stitch is designed to hem fabrics so that the stitches are almost invisible when looked at from the right side of the garment.

BASIC TECHNIQUES
Here are some basic techniques used throughout this book. They apply to both hand- and machine-sewing.

Hemming: When hemming a garment, make sure you turn over the edge twice so that no raw edge shows; this will prevent fraying and loose threads from hanging down. Pin in place and press before sewing with a machine or by hand.

Elasticated waistbands: Creating an elasticated waistband is very similar to hemming a garment – simply turn the fabric over twice to create a casing wide enough for your elastic, then pin and stitch, making sure to leave a gap to thread the elastic through. A knitting needle, chopstick or pen can be used to push the elastic through the waistband. Sew the ends of the elastic together, then stitch the gap in the waistband closed.

Darts: These are used to tailor the fit of a garment by taking fabric in at places on the garment, and are most often used in the waistband and bust of dresses and skirts. They are done by folding the fabric flat and beginning to sew the dart at the edge of the seam allowance to a point. A few stitches from the point, shorten the stitch length.

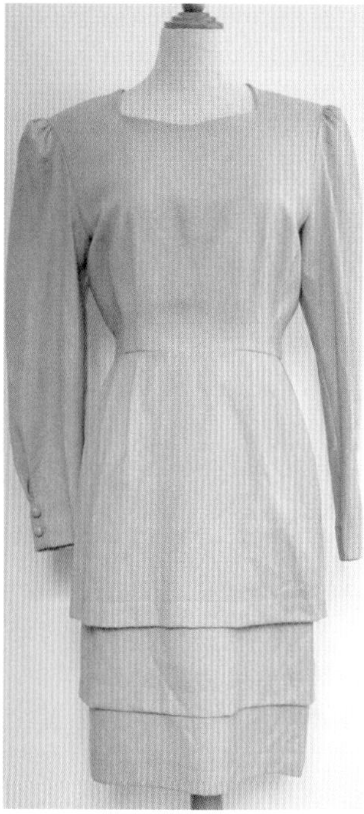
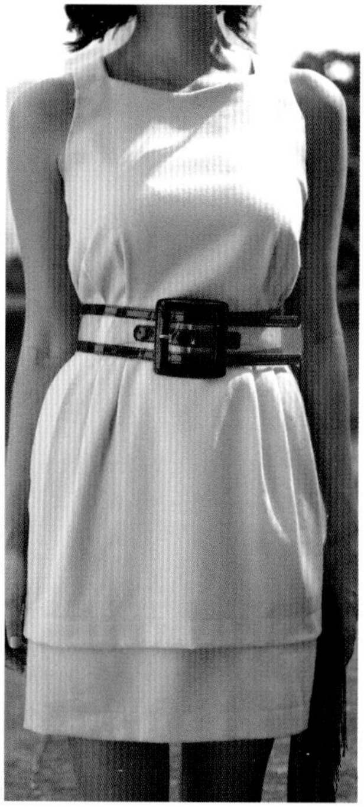
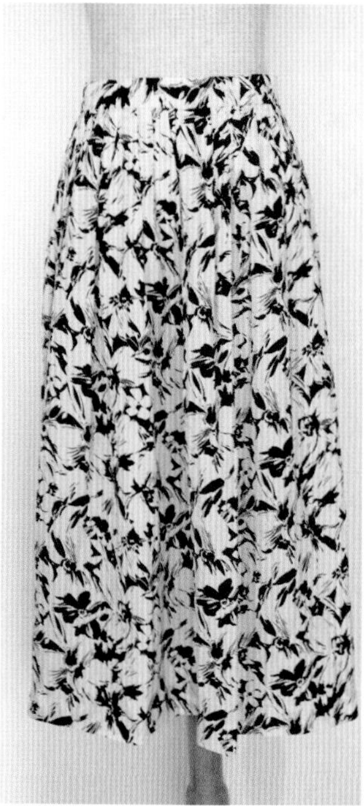
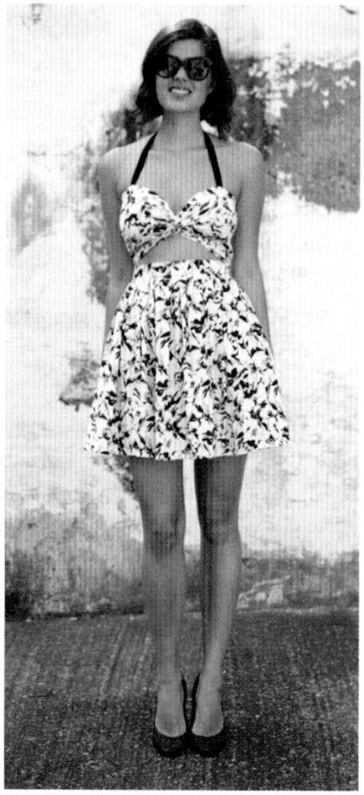
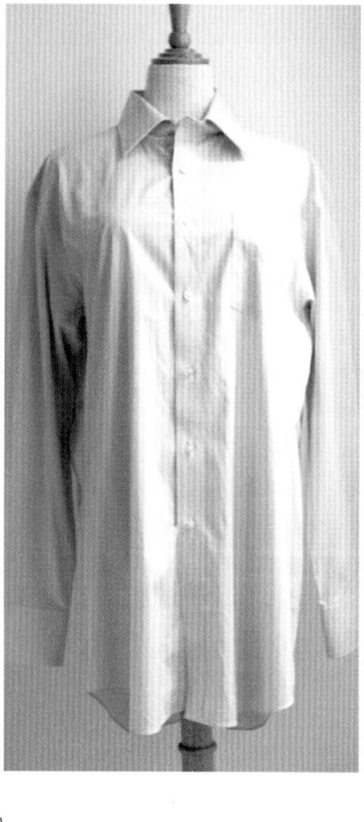
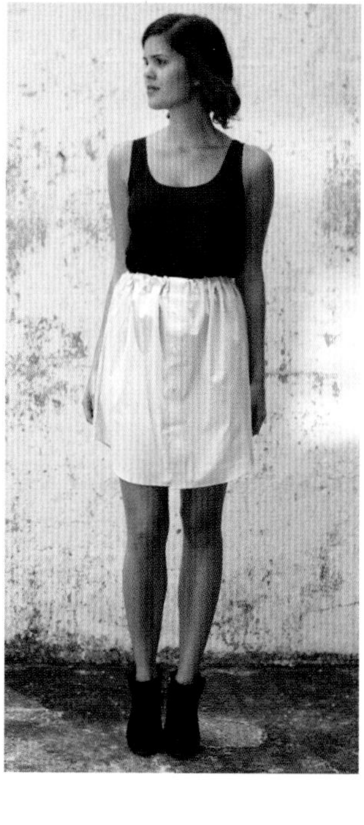
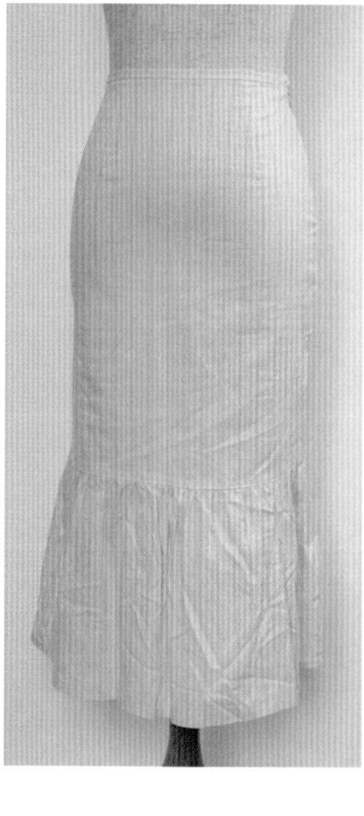
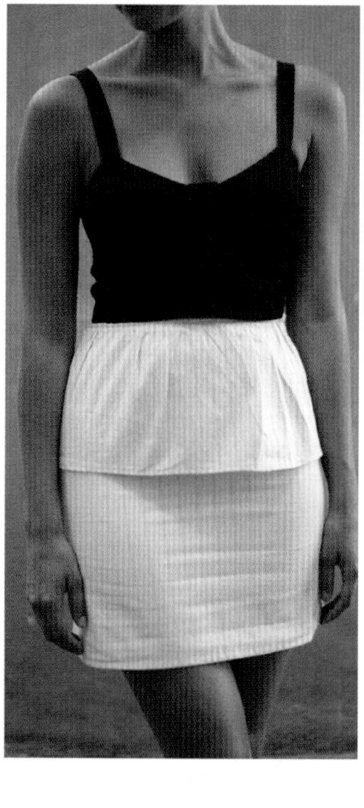

BEFORE & AFTER PROJECTS

Ever since I was very young, I've had a fascination with anything that involves an element of before-and-after – Cinderella-like transformations have always intrigued me, whether they're in the form of a makeover or a home renovation. For me, some of the most satisfying DIY projects involve reworking secondhand pieces that are outdated or just plain unattractive into gorgeous and on-trend items that become wardrobe favourites. I've been doing this since I was a child, and through trial and error I've come up with a few tips for getting the most out of all sorts of thrifted and vintage pieces that you may find.

In this section I've included a few of my favourite before-and-after projects for you to re-create. A printed skirt becomes a gorgeous summer cut-out dress, an oversized black shift dress is reworked into a sexy backless number and a men's shirt is transformed into a stylish summer skirt.

A GUIDE TO BEFORE & AFTER PROJECTS

GET INSPIRED. Take inspiration from fashion magazines, catwalk collections, street looks and other mediums to continually create ideas for what to do with the secondhand pieces you find. By taking current ideas off the catwalk and applying them to secondhand pieces, you'll be able to look fashionable without breaking the bank.

KNOW YOUR FABRICS. When buying secondhand, seek out the best fabrics you can find: natural fabrics such as silks, good-quality cottons and wool, as well as handmade fabrics that feel nice against the skin. If you can't tell just from looking or feeling, check the fabric tag.

PRINT, PATTERNS AND COLOUR. When scanning a big rack of clothes, keep your eyes peeled for evocative fabrics that catch your eye. My most successful reconstruction projects have been finding ill-fitting pieces that have beautiful patterns, and turning them into something gorgeous and well-fitting.

ADJUST THE SILHOUETTE. Following the waistline is a great way to achieve a modern look for an old piece of clothing. Insert darts into dresses, skirt or shirts to make them fit well at the waist and look amazing.

LOOK AT THE COMPONENT PARTS AS WELL AS THE WHOLE. Garments are often made up of a number of different pieces: dresses may comprise a skirt and a top, while shirts have front panels, a collar and sleeves. When you're looking at a thrifted piece for before-and-after potential, try to break down the garment into its component parts and think about how you could use the various pieces.

CHANGE THE LENGTH. Altering the length of an item will instantly update its look or even radically change it. You can turn a pair of trousers into shorts, cut a skirt to make a mini or even add length by sewing on fabric. You'll be amazed at how different the item will look.

EMBELLISH. Update your item by studding, beading, adding lace, fringe or just about anything else you can think of. You can also dye your garment to give it a completely new look.

PAY ATTENTION TO THE FINISH. Attention to detail in terms of the finishing of a garment, like sewing hems properly and ensuring no rough edges are showing, is one of the most important things that will take your projects from looking homemade to designer perfection.

REWORKED PARTY DRESS

Time: 1 hour

Skill Level: ✂ ✂ ✂ ✂

While on secondhand store adventures, you will no doubt come across all types of clothing, from various eras, countries and trends. You may often be overwhelmed by how unfashionable some items are, and wonder who in their right mind would have worn it, and where.

Stemming from a lifetime of trying to make secondhand clothes "cool", I now view these pieces as a challenge, because it's my belief that within all unattractive garments lies something that can be salvaged and, hopefully, turned into a standout piece for your wardrobe. To demonstrate how it is indeed possible to resurrect even the most unsightly garment using a little time and elbow grease, I have given this project what I would call an "extreme makeover". A seemingly unwearable dress – baby pink with puffed oversized sleeves and an odd tiered length – has been turned into a perfectly fitting dress that wouldn't look out of place at a summer cocktail party.

Wear It: Accessorize this chic party dress with sky-high heels and a clutch. Throw over a sequinned jacket to take the ensemble into the night.

Tip: When tackling these sorts of dress projects, it helps to follow the formula: length, shoulders, waist. Look at these three elements one at a time and if they are not modern or on-trend, think how they can be updated. Once you feel that all three elements are up to scratch, chances are you'll have a wearable piece.

Tip: I used a dressmaker's dummy for making this project. However you can just as easily pin the dress on yourself, removing it to do the alterations. You will need to know your exact measurements so that you can adjust the fit to suit your body.

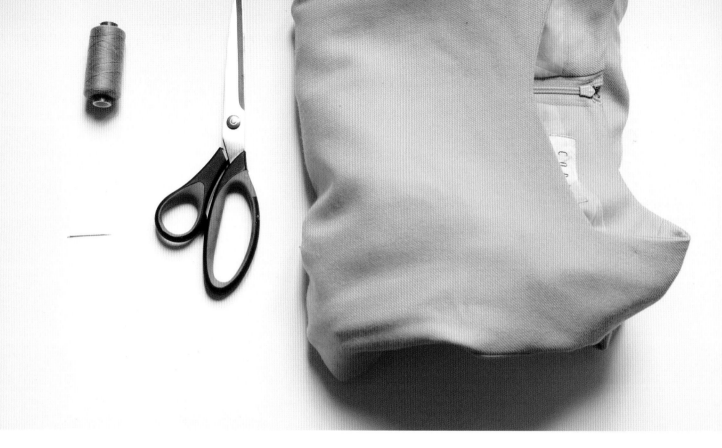

You Will Need:

- Secondhand dress
- Scissors
- Pins
- Tape measure
- Sewing machine or needle and thread

How To:

1. Length

Update the length of the dress to a more flattering style. This dress had three tiered sections, so the bottom tier was removed to create a more flattering mini length.

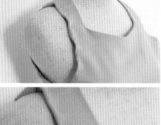

2. Shoulders

This dress had shoulderpads and flouncy sleeves. First the shoulderpads were removed and then the sleeves were carefully unpicked at the seams with a seam ripper. A needle and thread was used to hand-sew the edge of the shoulder seams under to create shoulder straps.

3. Waist

Now create a more flattering waistline. Turn the dress inside-out, pinning the dress to follow your waist measurements and then hand- or machine-stitch new seams. Make sure you take in the same amount along both side seams. If your dress has lining, like mine did, make sure you alter it at the same time as the outside shell of the dress.

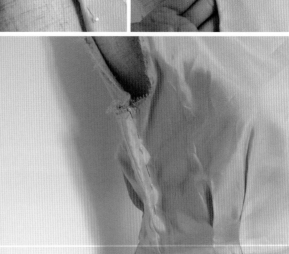

"PERFECT LENGTH" LEATHER SKIRT

Time: 1 hour, plus drying time

Skill Level: ✂ ✂

Leather skirts are one item that never seem to go out of fashion, and if they do, it's not long before they are back on the radar again. Unfortunately, the perfect leather skirt can be difficult and often costly to find. Finding a version that's the right length – for me, midway between thigh and knee – is almost impossible. That's where DIY can be a lifesaver, allowing you to customize a secondhand piece to look exactly as you'd like.

If you spend as much time in charity shops as I do, you will be aware that they nearly always have a leather skirt or two for sale. In most cases these have been cast off due to their unflattering length. Although it may seem that these pieces hanging sadly on the rail are a lost cause, with a little time and elbow grease you can turn them into a cornerstone of your wardrobe.

Interestingly, customizing a leather skirt into exactly what you want is easier than you think. Have you ever noticed that leather hems are rarely stitched? The technique I will show you, of cutting and gluing hems, is almost exactly the same as designers and manufacturers use when they work with leather.

Wear It: This style of skirt works well when paired with understated separates such as a vintage blouse and heels for a night out, or a nautical striped T-shirt and flat pumps for a more casual, daytime look.

Tip: Fabric glue can be used to secure hems on all leather projects, including creating shorts out of trousers and re-gluing a detached hem.

Tip: Look for a skirt that fits you well around the waist, as it is much harder to adjust the waist size than it is to change the length.

- Secondhand leather skirt
- Scissors
- Tape measure
- Pins
- Tailor's chalk
- Fabric or leather glue

How To:

1.
Put the leather skirt on and mark the new length you want it to be with tailor's chalk. Take off the skirt and mark out a straight line to follow when cutting, adding an extra 2.5 cm (1 in) to your chosen length for the hem.

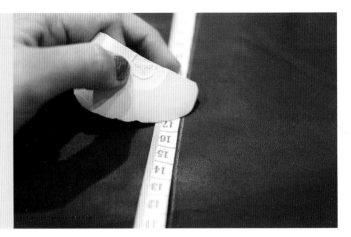

2.

Cut the skirt to length using scissors.

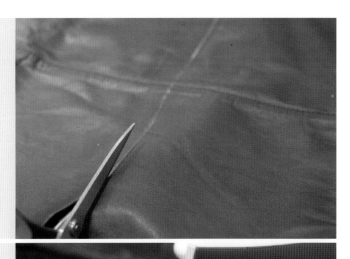

3.

Turn the skirt inside out, then turn over the edge by 2.5 cm (1 in) to create a clean hem. Press down with an iron set to a low temperature. Pin in place.

4.

To secure the hem in place, apply the glue under the hem and pressdown firmly. Weigh the skirt down with heavy books while the glue dries overnight.

PEPLUM SKIRT

Time: 1 hour

Skill Level: ✂ ✂ ✂ ✂

For the last few years the peplum silhouette has been incredibly popular. When it first emerged in the nineteenth century, the peplum was an accessory that was put over the top of an outfit, but these days you will most often find it attached to dresses, skirts or jackets. For me, the peplum skirt is one of those hard-working pieces that is ideal for work and equally appropriate dressed up for a night out.

Although peplums are traditionally created by attaching a doughnut-shaped piece of fabric to the waistband by its inner edge, this can be time-consuming and tricky to do at home. So in this project I will show you a very simple way to create one using a secondhand flared or ruffle-hem skirt.

The project involves taking off the flared or ruffled section at the bottom of the skirt and stitching it to the waistband. It honestly couldn't be easier and has a stylish result that will integrate perfectly into your everyday wardrobe.

Wear It: Emphasize an hourglass silhouette by pairing the peplum skirt with a fitted top, such as a long-sleeved, figure-hugging jersey.

Tip: *For this project you can use any type of flared or ruffle-hem skirt; just make sure the ruffled section has enough volume to create a noticeable peplum look.*

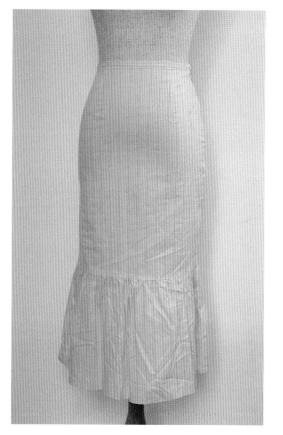

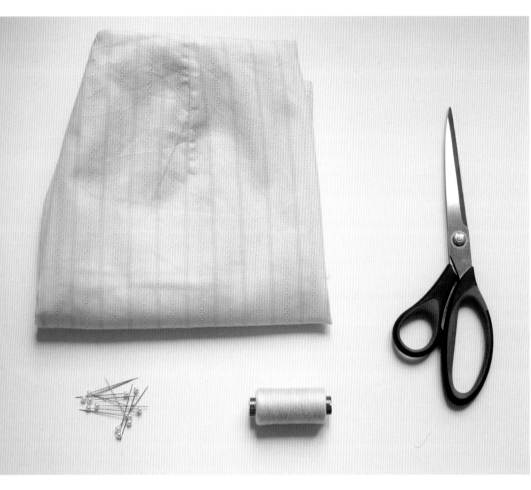

You Will Need:

- Secondhand skirt with a flared or ruffled hem
- Scissors
- Pins
- Tape measure
- Sewing machine or needle and thread

How To:

1.
Remove the flared bottom ruffle of the skirt by cutting close to the seam edge. Unpick any seams, as necessary, so that you don't damage either section of the skirt and cause fraying. If your skirt has a lining, cut this to the same dimensions as the base skirt.

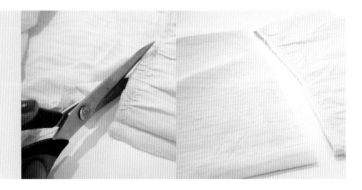

2.

If the base skirt is too long, cut it to your desired length, plus an extra 2 cm (¾ in) for hemming. Turn under the raw edge twice to create a narrow hem, and pin in place. Stitch by machine, using a straight stitch, or by hand. If your skirt has a lining, hem the lining separately in the same way, making sure the lining is 1 cm (¼ inch) shorter than the length of the skirt.

3.

For the peplum section, unpick one of the side seams to create one long piece of fabric.

4.

Pin the peplum piece to the waistband of the base skirt, making sure to orientate the open side of the peplum with the zip opening. If you think the peplum is too long, remove it and cut it shorter, re-hemming as in step 2.

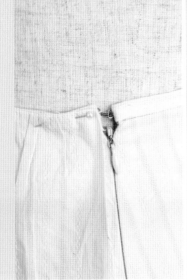

5.

Sew the peplum in place along the edge of the waistband, using a straight stitch on a sewing machine or by hand.

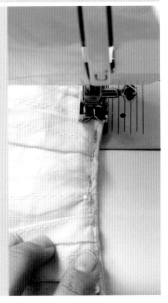

BOYFRIEND-SHIRT SKIRT

Time: 1 hour

Skill Level: ✂ ✂ ✂ ✂

Possibly the most frequently stumbled-upon piece of clothing in any second-hand store is the men's shirt. Although most of us overlook them, believing there is nothing you can do to change them, it seems a shame not to turn these dull items into something chic and wearable, especially given that they often come in luxurious fabrics and interesting prints. In reality, there are a huge number of things you can do to rework a men's shirt, from creating a chic statement collar to turning it into a sleeveless dress. Whenever I see a men's shirt in a fun pattern or print, or even sometimes a plain white one, I always snap it up, knowing that I will find a use for it in the future.

   For this project I used a lilac shirt that had been overlooked by all the other secondhand-store-savvy fashionistas. I chose it because I knew the pastel colour would look gorgeous as a skirt. The key to these types of projects is seeing the opportunity in a print, pattern or shape hanging on a rack and imagining how it could be reinvented to become a key piece in your wardrobe.

Wear It: Pair this simple style with a silk camisole and some suede boots or black heeled pumps.

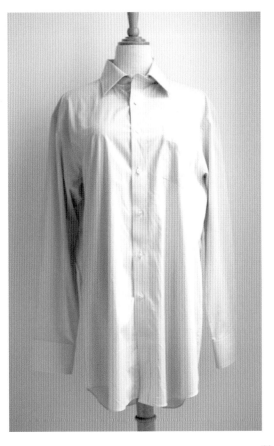

Tip: Look for a shirt that is oversized so that you have more volume in the skirt.

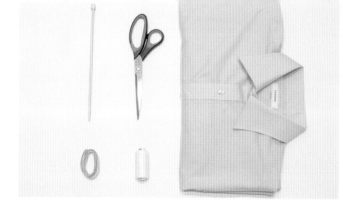

You Will Need:

- Oversized men's shirt
- 2.5 cm (1 in) wide elastic, length to fit your waist
- Tape measure
- Scissors
- Pins
- Sewing machine or needle and thread

How To:

1.

Cut the top off the shirt underneath the arms, measuring and marking to ensure a straight line. Discard the top half – you will only be using the bottom section. It is fine to cut through any pockets, but if you prefer, unpick the pockets and remove them. If you do this, first make sure they won't leave a mark behind.

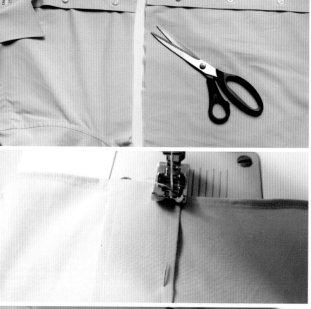

2.

With the skirt piece buttoned up, pin the button strip along the long edge through both layers of fabric. Stitch along the long edges, either by hand or with a machine, to permanently secure the front panels of the fabric together.

3.

Turn over a small hem along the top raw edge and stitch in place to finish off.

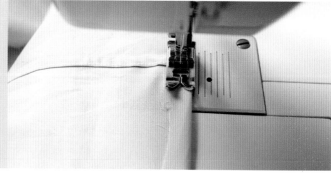

4.
Create a waistband casing through which to thread the elastic. Turn over the top raw edge of fabric to the wrong side, folding under to a depth of 5 cm (2 in). Press.

5.
Hand- or machine-sew the waistband casing, making sure you leave a gap to feed the elastic through.

6.
Measure and cut the elastic to fit your waist, allowing a small overlap to stitch the two short ends together. Now thread the elastic onto a knitting needle or pen and push the elastic through the waistband, gathering up the fabric as you go.

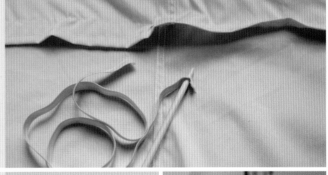

7.
Once all the fabric has been gathered onto the elastic, sew the elastic ends together to secure. Stitch the gap in the waistband closed.

BACKLESS LITTLE BLACK DRESS

Time: 2 hours

Skill Level: ✂ ✂ ✂ ✂

Polished but with a youthful twist, there's nothing more feminine than a backless LBD, a style that every woman should have in her closet. Often seen on the red carpet and catwalk, the cut-out dress shows a subtle hint of a tanned back. Fortunately, the backless dress is a relatively simple project to make at home using a secondhand shift dress, and what's even better is that you can tailor the cut-out style to your body shape, ensuring that the dress looks great on you, and you will feel equally amazing while wearing it.

To make this dress, I converted a standard black shift dress by shortening the hem as well as cutting out the back, so be sure to look at all types of dresses in your local secondhand store and change the length if required.

Wear It: Pair your backless dress with sky-high heels and a nude clutch for a standout cocktail look.

Tip: When looking for a suitable dress for this project, choose one that has a zip in the back and a hook-and-eye fastening at the nape of the neck above the zip.

Tip: To make sure you get the cut-out of the dress just right, work slowly and cut less than required at first. It's always easy to trim away excess if you need to, but it's virtually impossibly to re-attach fabric once cut.

You Will Need:

- Black shift dress
- Scissors
- Pins
- Needle and thread or sewing machine
- Tailor's chalk
- Ruler or tape measure

How To:

1.

If necessary, shorten the skirt by cutting it to the required length, adding on 2.5 cm (1 in) for the hem.

2.

Turn under the hem. Pin in place and stitch, by hand or machine. You now have a mini dress to use as the base of the project.

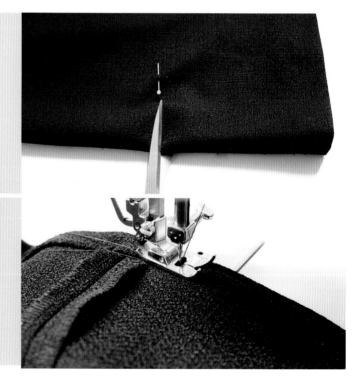

3.

Using tailor's chalk, draw the cut-out section onto the right-side of the fabric on the back of the dress. You can do this on a flat table or on a dressmaker's dummy. Here we cut an oval shape from the centre neck to the lower centre back but you can make any shape you prefer. Measure carefully with a ruler to ensure your shape is symmetrical.

4.

Now pull the zip down to below where you want the cut the dress out. Ensure you leave 2.5 cm (1 in) at the neckline for a hook-and-eye closure before you cut. Now cut out the shape, following the chalk lines.

5.

Turn over the raw edges of the cut-line by 2.5 cm (1 in) and pin in place. Sew by hand to hem or machine topstitch on the right side of the fabric.

GARDEN PARTY SUMMER DRESS

Time: 1 hour

Skill Level: ✂ ✂ ✂ ✂

The key to before-and-after projects is your ability to see the opportunity in a print or pattern and to imagine how you could turn the item into something beautiful and elegant. It's important to think about how an item could look if deconstructed, and how a print can be altered when displayed in a different way. I was drawn to the floral monotone print of a calf-length silk skirt (the "before" in this project), but knew that it wouldn't fit into my wardrobe as it was, so I thought I could turn it into a dress. This is one of those projects that works with just about every calf-length skirt you see and it's just a matter of matching a halter-strap to the style.

Wear It: This cut-out style is ideal for a garden party or relaxed wedding, so pair it with low-key accessories and a pair of strappy heels.

Tip: When you look for a "before" skirt for this project, choose one that is full and has extra fabric in the width, so there is enough to create the top piece.

Tip: To determine where to attach the ribbon strap, wrap the top on you without the ribbon, then pin the ribbon in place.

You Will Need:

- Calf-length skirt in a summery pattern
- 2.5 cm (1 in) wide ribbon, about 50 cm (20 in) in length
- Pins
- Tape measure
- Scissors
- Sewing machine or needle and thread

1.

Try the skirt on, then mark the length you want the dress to be with pins. Add an extra 2.5 cm (1 in) for turning under the hem, then cut to length.

2.

You will now have a basic mini skirt, plus enough surplus fabric for the top piece, which will become the bodice of the dress. Turn over the raw edge on the mini skirt by 2.5 cm (1 in), then pin and stitch in place by hand or machine.

3.

Cut the surplus fabric piece along one seam to create a single length of fabric. Hem the cut edges of the fabric by turning over 2.5 cm (1 in) and sewing in place. To attach the halter strap, wrap the top first (as shown in steps 4–7) to decide where to attach the two ends, and then pin and sew the ribbon in place.

4.

To wrap the top, place the centre of the fabric behind you with the two ends on either side and slip your arms through the halter.

5.

Bring the both ends in front of you to cover the breasts tightly and twist together at the centre, between the breasts.

6.

Then take the fabric around to the back and tie in a bow.

7.

Put the skirt over the top to form a dress style with a triangular cut out.

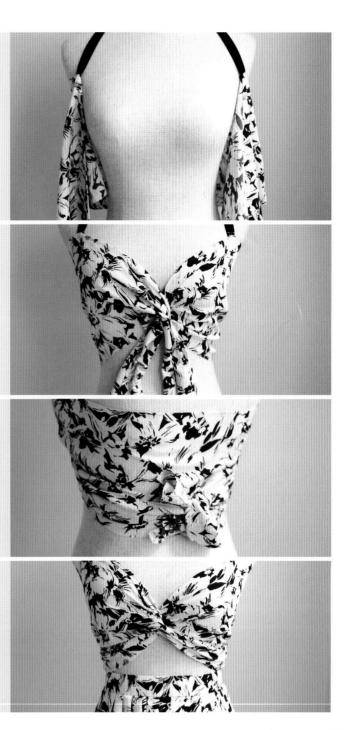

SLEEVELESS JACKET

Time: 1 hour

Skill Level: ✂ ✂ ✂ ✂

A sleeveless jacket is an incredibly versatile piece that integrates perfectly into any wardrobe, particularly during the trans-seasonal Spring and Autumn months when the weather is changing. Sleeveless styles can be reworked using a secondhand jacket, and are a great idea when you find one that doesn't quite fit. Thrift and charity shops are full of jackets with oversized and ill-fitting shoulders and sleeves, which can be reworked into chic sleeveless jackets or gilets. For this project, the steps involved are so simple that you are guaranteed to go from frumpy to chic in a matter of minutes.

Wear It: Pair with jeans or a mini skirt for a stylish summer look, or layer with a knit on cooler days.

Tip: Take your time stitching around the armholes, as these can be a little trickier than your average straight-line sewing. For a professional-looking finish, take it slow and hand-stitch carefully.

You Will Need:

- Oversized jacket
- Scissors
- Seam ripper/unpicker
- Pins
- Matching thread
- Needle or sewing machine

How To:

1.
Remove the shoulder pads if your jacket has them – keep them in case you want to use them in future projects.

2.
Using a seam ripper, remove the stitching that attaches the sleeves to the shoulders. Snip any stray threads.

3.
Press the raw jacket edges flat.

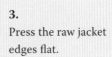

4.
Roll the edges of the jacket armhole over on the underside of the fabric twice so that no raw edge is exposed, then pin in place and press. If your blazer has lining, do both layers of fabric together.

5.
Either by hand or with a sewing machine, stitch along the new edge. If stitching by hand, use fine stitches on the outside and longer stitches on the inside to give you an invisible arm seam.

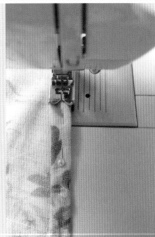

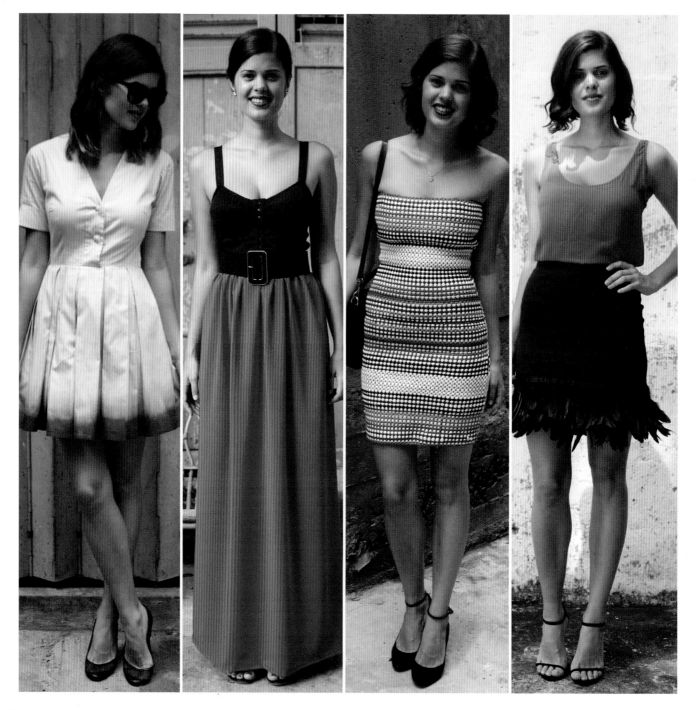

DRESSES & SKIRTS

Dresses and skirts are the ultimate in feminine dressing. Luckily, there are so many ways for you to use DIY to create endless varieties. In this section you'll learn how to make a one-shoulder dress using a genius wrapping technique, sew a sexy bodycon dress out of rugs (yes, really!), use a dip-dyeing technique to create a chic day dress and customize a skirt by trimming it with feathers.

DIP-DYED PASTEL DRESS

Time: 1 hour, plus drying time

Skill Level: ✂ ✂

I have a love of reinventing dresses found in secondhand shops and turning them into contemporary pieces. One of my favourite techniques is using dye to change the colour and look of the item.

In the last few years, the dip-dye trend has become popular across the world. First seen in the hair of Japanese girls in the Harajuku district of Tokyo, the look quickly became mainstream. It has since been used in clothes in designer collections, on dresses, skirts and tops. Creating dip-dyed pieces yourself really couldn't be easier – it just involves carefully dipping your item into dye while making sure not to get dye anywhere else on the fabric. In this project, a vintage cotton dress has been transformed using this technique.

Wear It: Match the dress with black accessories to emphasize the colourful section of the dress.

Tip: If you don't have an outdoor area in which to do this project, place the bucket in your shower or bath so that you don't splash dye on the floor.

Tip: Take your time when dip-dying and always dip less of the dress than you first think you need to. You can always go back and dip more later.

Tip: Always test the dye mixture with a square of surplus fabric first; this way you can see how quickly the fabric will absorb the dye and also the concentration of colour you want to achieve.

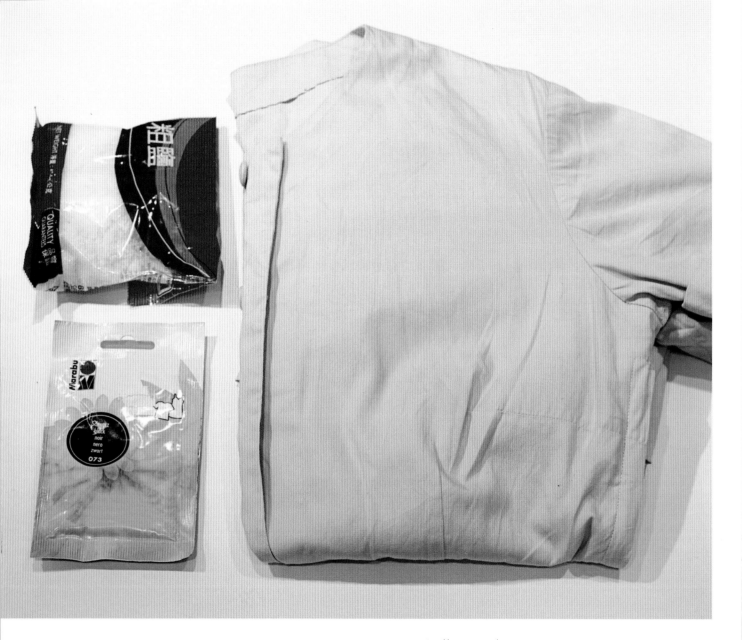

You Will Need:

- Pastel cotton dress
- Clothes hanger
- 50 g (1¾ oz) pack black hand dye
- Bucket
- 250 g (5 tbsp) salt, or as recommended by the dye manufacturer

How To:

1.

Wash your dress first, then let it dry. Place the dress on a hanger and dampen the bottom 25 cm (10 in) of the dress. You want it to be wet but not dripping – this helps the fabric take on the dye evenly.

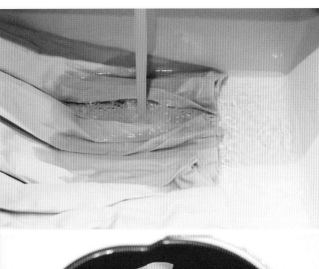

2.

Fill the bucket with very hot water and add the dye, following the instructions on the pack. Add salt as instructed; this will help the dye to set. Stir.

3.

Dip around 10 cm (4 in) of the bottom of the dress into the dye, making sure it is level so that the dye line is straight. Leave the dress to take colour for approximately 30 minutes. Remove the dress from the dye and hang it up outside or over the bathtub to dry. Once dry, rinse it in the washing machine or set the dye as instructed on the pack.

RUG BODYCON DRESS

Time: 1 hour

Skill Level: ✂ ✂ ✂ ✂ ✂

"Bodycon", or body-conscious styles, were hugely popular in the early 1990s and have continued to be a trend that fashionistas all over the world embrace. When made out of the right type of thick stretchy material, these dresses flatter the figure and can be worn underneath other layers.

I've always enjoyed rummaging in my local homeware store to see if they have any inexpensive materials I can use for my next project. One of my most treasured finds was inexpensive stretchy rugs. Made from recycled jersey T-shirt offcuts, they make a form-fitting fabric for a chic and stylish bodycon dress. For me, this project is the ultimate proof that you needn't sacrifice your budget to wear something unique, and it shows that you can feel great while wearing something as mundane as a refashioned rug!

The pattern for the dress is created from a dress you already own – choose one in a similar fabric to ensure the sizing is generally the same.

Wear It: Layer this dress underneath a white silk shirt or wear it on its own with wedge heels for a perfect party look.

Tip: A simple exposed zip was sewn on the outside of the dress, but use an invisible zip if you prefer.

Tip: Look in your local homeware stores for these types of stretchy rugs. Chinese-owned stores may be more likely to stock them.

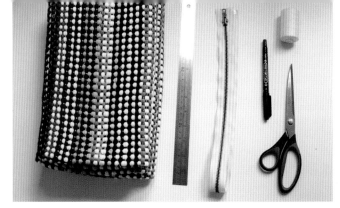

You Will Need:

- 4 stretchy rugs, measuring approximately 40 cm (16 in) long and 80 cm (32 in) wide
- Needle and thread
- Pins
- Scissors

- 60 cm (24 in) white open-end zip
- Sewing machine, with a heavy-duty denim needle
- Bodycon dress, as a pattern
- Craft paper
- Ruler
- Black marker pen

How To:

1.
On the wrong side of the fabric, hand-stitch two of the rugs together along their long edges to join the pieces and create one large square of fabric. Repeat with the other two rugs. You now have one square for the back and another for the front.

2.
To create the exposed zip, place a rug square with the banding running horizontally and pin the zip down the centre on the right side. Machine-stitch along both long edges and around the bottom of the zip.

3.
Using the scissors and working on the wrong side of fabric, cut down the centre length of the zip to create the opening.

4.
Now snip into the fabric between the two rows of stitching to expose the zip fully and allow it to open and close. Trim the fabric away from the inside of the zip so the cloth will not get caught in the teeth.

5.

Now make a paper pattern. Place your bodycon dress on the craft paper and trace around the shape and then cut out, adding 2.5 cm (1 in) for the side seams only. Fold the pattern in half to make sure it is symmetrical and trim if required.

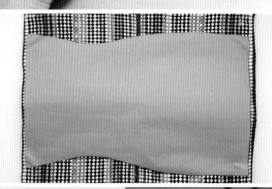

6.

Pin the two pieces of rug fabric together with right sides facing and the zip on the inside. Pin the pattern onto the rug fabric through both thicknesses.

7.

Trace around the sides of the pattern onto the fabric with the marker pen. Retain the top and the bottom of the rugs as the top and the bottom hems of the dress.

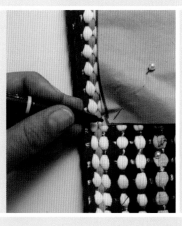

8.

Remove the pattern and machine-stitch along the pen lines.

9.

Cut along the sewn edges of the fabric to create the dress. Then turn right sides out.

CLASSIC MAXI SKIRT

Time: 1 hour

Skill Level: ✂ ✂ ✂ ✂

A maxi skirt is one item of clothing that I consider to be a wardrobe essential, regardless of your age, style or body shape. Not only does it feel fantastic to wear, it also hides all manner of body flaws and is the perfect item to throw on when you want a simple yet stylish outfit.

In the past, the maxi length was mostly seen in formal dresses and bohemian-style pieces. However, this style has now become central to any functional and wearable wardrobe. Season after season, floor-grazing lengths have been seen on the catwalk in prints, bright colours and luxurious fabrics. Designer collections have shown that the maxi length is appropriate for all occasions, from the beach to the bar, and even to the boardroom.

Not purely confined to summer, a maxi can be worn over leggings with a belted knit during winter as well as with gladiator flats and a strappy top during the warmer months. The maxi is clearly a year-round staple – and so simple to make!

Wear It: Wear your maxi skirt with flat sandals and a strappy top. Layer a belt over the elasticated waistband for a more elegant look.

Tip: *When choosing fabric for this project, try to buy some that is approximately 5 cm (10 inches) wider than your desired maxi length, so you can use a single panel of fabric.*

Tip: *The technique used to make the skirt can also be used to make mini and mid-length skirts.*

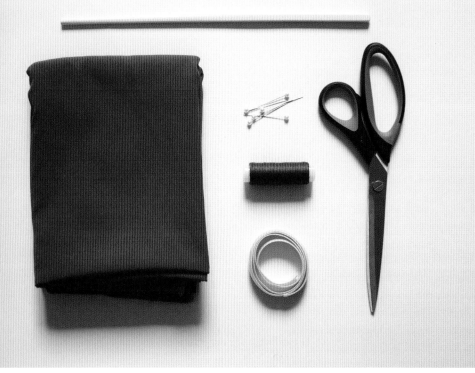

You Will Need:

- 2 m (80 in) length x 150 cm (60 in) wide cotton or silk fabric
- 2.5 cm (1 in) wide elastic, length to fit your waist
- Pins
- Sewing machine or needle and thread
- Tape measure
- Scissors
- Knitting needle or pen

How To:

1.
Press the fabric. Then, along one of the long edges, turn over and pin 3 cm (1¼ in) to create the casing for the elastic waistband.

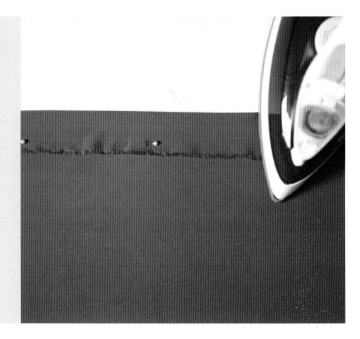

2.

Stitch along the pinned
edge. Then fold the fabric
lengthwise, right sides
together, and pin and
stitch the skirt side seam
from hem to just below
the waistband casing.

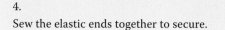

3.

Measure and cut the elastic
to fit your waist. Using a
knitting needle or pen,
push the elastic through the
waistband casing, gathering
as you go.

4.

Sew the elastic ends together to secure.

5.

Stitch the gap to close the waistband.

6.

Try the skirt on and measure and mark to the desired length,
plus an extra 2.5 cm (1 in). The ideal length will graze the
top of the foot. To hem, turn the edge over twice and pin
and stitch by hand or machine.

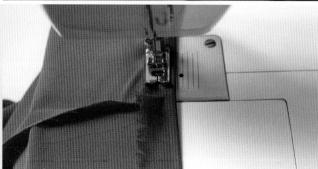

LEOPARD-PRINT WRAP DRESS

Time: 1 hour

Skill Level: ✂ ✂ ✂

An asymmetric style that covers one shoulder and leaves the other bare is both sexy and elegant. This beautiful wrap dress is incredibly simple to make and suits women of all shapes and sizes. It can be assembled with any mixture of fabrics and is just as gorgeous in block colours and prints as it is in classic black. From the off-the-shoulder cut to the figure-flattering fit, this is a useful piece that will never go out of fashion.

It may take you a few tries to get the wrapping and gathering exactly as you like, but play around with the fabric to suit your style and frame. Make sure you cover the top of the waistband of the skirt with the wrapped fabric for a streamlined look.

Wear It: Romantic with a directional edge, this piece is best teamed with a pair of extremely high heels and black accents for a look that redefines after-dark standards.

Tip: *To finish, secure with a few stitches to keep the wrapped top held together; unpick to remove.*

You Will Need:

- 2 m (80 in) leopard-print fabric, approximately 30 cm (12 in) wide

- Premade mini or maxi skirt made in the same way as the skirt on pages 62–5
- Scissors
- Needle and thread

How To:

1.

Hem any raw edges on the strip of fabric then place it over your right shoulder with the short end in front and the rest of the length behind you. Tuck the short end into the skirt.

2.

Twist and tighten the fabric over the right shoulder, making sure to cover your breast properly.

3.

Keep twisting and take the fabric around your back and under your left arm.

4.

Bring the fabric across the front horizontally to cover your left breast.

5.

Bring the fabric around tightly behind your back again, wrapping around the waist.

6.

Keep wrapping tightly around the torso until you have run out of fabric. When this happens tuck the end into the wrapped fabric and secure with a few stitches.

FEATHER-HEM SKIRT

Time: 1 hour

Skill Level: ✂ ✂ ✂ ✂

Never underestimate the effect of embellished hems. Feathers have such a luxurious feel and can take a plain mini skirt from "blah" to anything but in a matter of moments. There's nothing more satisfying than taking an item that's been languishing in your closet, like a plain black skirt, and using crafting techniques to turn it into something integral to your wardrobe. In this case, the addition of feather embellishments to the hem of a secondhand mini skirt completely changes the look and feel of the piece, turning it into something chic and expensive-looking.

Wear It: Team this statement-making style with simple accessories – a coloured tank, a stack of silver bangles and strappy sandals are all you need.

Tip: If you are having trouble finding feather trim in your local craft store or haberdashery, look at online craft stores which are likely to have a greater selection.

Tip: The perfect mini skirt can sometimes be a challenge to find, so one option is to search your local secondhand shop for a plain pencil skirt and shorten it into a mini – customized to the exact length just for you!

You Will Need:

- Black mini skirt
- Pins
- Needle and thread or sewing machine

- Two lengths of feather trim, slightly longer than the length around the hem of mini skirt

How To:

1.
Ensure the mini skirt is the length you want and shorten it if necessary.

2.
Pin a layer of the feather trim directly onto the right side of the skirt, approximately 5 cm (2 in) from the hem.

3.
Pin another layer on top of the first, approximately 2.5 cm (1 in) above the first. Hold up and check that the feather trim falls to the length you desire – here the trim falls to approximately 15 cm (6 in) above the knee.

4.
Hand- or machine-stitch the fringing onto the skirt, one layer at a time, using a topstitch. Fold the top layer up while stitching the underneath layer.

TOPS & JACKETS

Stylish tops are essential in any fashionista's wardrobe, and a gorgeous blouse takes an outfit from ordinary to extraordinary in a matter of moments. Although many of us opt for classic tops to complement the rest of our wardrobe, there's no reason why a beautifully embellished or reworked top should not be the centrepiece of an outfit. The options – in terms of putting a creative spin on your basic pieces – are endless for the DIY enthusiast, and in this section I show you some of my all-time favourite projects to get you started. The split-sleeve nautical top and leather-trimmed denim shirt lend themselves to casual weekend outfits, while the fringed tassel top is perfect for festivals and parties.

CUT-OUT NAUTICAL TOP

Time: 1 hour

Skill Level: ✂ ✂ ✂ ✂

No fashionista's wardrobe would be complete without at least one nautical-style top – a T-shirt with long sleeves and horizontal navy and white stripes. Originally the uniform of French sailors, it is said that Coco Chanel was so taken by the Breton shirts worn by the fishermen in the French Riviera that she brought the stripes to the catwalk – and her own wardrobe – soon after. The nautical-style top is the uniform of both chic artists and jet-setting girls alike, lending a casual yet elegant look to spring and summer outfits.

In this project a traditional nautical top is reworked by creating chic cut-outs, a small detail that reveals a bit of skin for an new take on a classic style.

Wear It: Emphasize the seafaring history of this top by pairing it with a white mini skirt or capri trousers, or modernize the look by donning wide-leg palazzo pants and ballet flats.

Tip: *Don't be confined to using this technique on just striped tops; it works just as well on block-colour styles and many other long-sleeved options.*

You Will Need:

- Striped long-sleeved T-shirt
- Scissors
- Pins
- 14 white buttons
- Tape measure
- 1.5 m (1¾ yd) of white polyester string
- White thread
- Sewing machine or needle and thread

How To:

1.
Press the T-shirt flat, creating a crease along the outer arm from shoulder to wrist. Make sure the crease is exactly the same on both sides. Using the crease as a guide, cut the shirt open along the arm. Hem the raw edges by turning them under twice, then pin in place and stitch by hand or machine.

2.
Cut 14 pieces of string 5 cm (2 in) long. These will be used to create the button loops for the arm closures.

3.
Sew the buttons in place down one side of the sleeve cut-outs. Use the stripes as a guide for placing the buttons, and space evenly. I placed a button every four stripes and used seven buttons per sleeve.

4.
To make the buttonholes, make loops out of the string pieces, pin in place on the underside of the edge of the fabric, opposite the buttons, and hand-stitch in place.

SHOULDERLESS SHIRT

Time: 1 hour

Skill Level: ✂ ✂ ✂

A classic white shirt never fails to lend an air of elegance and it's one of those pieces that works overtime in the wardrobe. Although the traditional white shirt is central to a variety of different outfits, a few strategically placed cut-outs can update the look.

Don't be worried about going crazy with your scissors – one of the reasons for buying secondhand clothing is to be able to experiment. In my many years of reworking and restyling clothing I've come to terms with the need to learn from trial and error. The first time I ever tried a cut-out (or "cold") shoulder, I cut far too much off the shoulders and ended up with huge holes and flapping sleeves. But because I only spent a tiny amount buying the shirt, and I could still use the collar for another project, it was a lesson well learnt. Luckily I have tried this project so many times now that I have come up with a foolproof method.

Wear It: Wear this cut-out shirt with high-waisted skirts or skinny jeans and heels.

Tip: This project is particularly useful if you have a shirt with shoulders that extend past your own – it removes the problematic bad fit completely.

Tip: To begin, cut out only a small section of fabric to create a subtle style. Even a small cut-out can change the overall hang of the garment, plus you can always cut more afterwards.

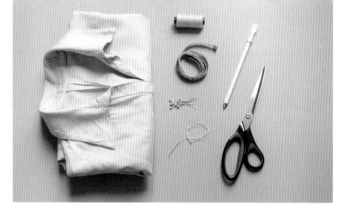

You Will Need:

- Long-sleeved collared shirt in silk or cotton
- Scissors
- Sewing needle and thread
- Tailor's chalk
- Pins
- Tape measure

How To:

1.
On the right shoulder, mark the off-the-shoulder area where you want the cut-out to start and finish with pins.

2.
Repeat on the left shoulder and use the tape measure to check that both sides are symmetrical and equal distance from the collar.

3.
On the right shoulder, mark the exact shape you want to cut out using pins and chalk. Cut out the marked shape with your scissors.

4.

Use this piece of fabric as a template to trace the shape on the left side, making sure to flip it over as a mirror image. Once both sides are cut out, check your progress by putting the shirt on and looking in a mirror. You may need to cut out more to get the right shape.

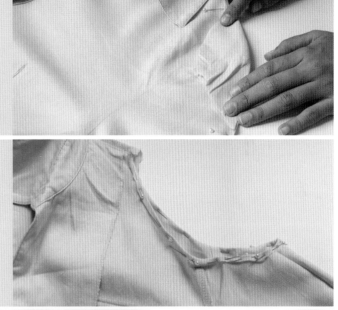

5.

With the wrong sides out, fold the raw edges of the cut-out section under twice, then press and pin in place.

6.

Hand-sew using small stitches on the right side and longer stitches on the underside.

7.

Press the stitched edge well to finish.

TASSEL-HEM TOP

Time: 45 minutes

Skill Level: ✂ ✂ ✂ ✂

Although the key to a wearable and functional wardrobe is a collection of classic items that make up a great number of outfits, everyone will have a few pieces that remind them of special times. For me, it's a black top with a fringe of black tassels around the hem. The tassels are such a fun detail that they never fail to get me twirling around, if only to see them spin with me. Items like these create a sense of spontaneity in the wardrobe and can enliven an outfit assembled of more classic pieces.

Wear It: This style, with its boho/hippie vibe, is perfect to wear to the beach in the summer. Because the top is midriff, you can pair it with a high-waisted skirt or over a dress to avoid showing skin. Alternatively, wear it with distressed denim shorts for a festival-appropriate look.

Tip: *For this project I machine-stitched the tassels on, but you can hand-sew them if you prefer.*

You Will Need:

- Black vest top
- 24 small black tassels, as used for soft furnishings
- Scissors
- Tape measure
- Black thread
- Sewing machine or needle and thread

How To:

1.
Measure, mark and cut the vest to midriff length, adding 2.5 cm (1 in) extra for the hem.

2.
With wrong sides out, turn under the raw edge and hem by hand or machine.

3.
Pin the tassels in place along the hem, making sure they are evenly spaced. I used two fingers – roughly 4 cm (1½ in) – to space them apart. Make sure that you leave a little bit of the hanging loop below the hem so that the tassels can "swing".

4.
Secure the loops of the tassels by hand or machine – use small stitches to ensure they are securely fastened.

5.
Snip off the looped ends of the tassels.

CHAIN PETER PAN TOP

Time: 1 hour

Skill Level: ✂ ✂ ✂

It can be difficult to find a top that is dressier than your average T-shirt yet more relaxed and trendy than a silk camisole. The right style can be like looking for a needle in a haystack. This is where DIY can be your best friend. It's the ideal method for getting what you want out of an outfit, allowing you to have control over what it looks like – while injecting some individuality into the style. These days I rarely try to shop for the perfect top and instead choose to make my own.

For this project I took a vintage long-sleeved shirt in a silk fabric and embellished it using black chain, which I bought inexpensively from my local craft store.

Wear It: Pair this collared top with a high-waisted leather skirt or brightly coloured mini skirt.

Tip: Choose lightweight chain for this project so that the silk shirt isn't weighed down by the embellishment, and feel free to experiment with colours and styles of chain. Gold or silver would look equally good.

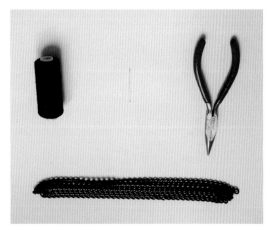

You Will Need:

- Collarless silk top or T-shirt
- 2 m (2¼ yd) black chain
- Scissors
- Pins
- Beading or needlenose pliers
- Needle and black thread

How To:

1.

Fold the chain in half and pin it to the collar where the shoulder seam meets the neckline on both sides of the shirt. Use the pliers to open and remove any links if necessary.

2.

Using the needle and thread, stitch the chain to both sides of the neckline. You will now have a chain that hangs like a necklace on the front of the shirt.

3.

Pin the uppermost length of chain to the centre front of the shirt on the seam, allowing the sides to drop down to create a Peter Pan collar shape. Stitch in place to secure.

4.

Repeat with the second length of chain, abutting it to the first, and secure in place with a few small stitches.

LEATHER COLLAR DENIM SHIRT

Time: 30 minutes, plus drying time

Skill Level: ✂ ✂

Nothing compares to a denim shirt for comfort and style, and the ease with which you are able to pair it with other items in your wardrobe. Fortunately denim shirts can always be found in secondhand stores, in both fitted and oversized versions. In this project I will show you how to update a basic shirt with a leather collar.

Wear It: Wear this chic collared shirt with a brightly coloured skirt or black skinny jeans.

Tip: Choose a flexible fabric glue that will allow some give in the bond. Experiment with other types of shirts for this project – any made from sturdy fabric, such as flannel, would work well.

You Will Need:

- Denim shirt with a collar
- Piece of leather, enough to cover the collar of the shirt
- Tailor's chalk
- Fabric glue
- Small paintbrush
- Scissors
- Ruler
- Foldback clips to hold in place while drying

How To:

1.

Trace the collar onto the back of the leather using tailor's chalk.

2.

Draw an extra 2.5 cm (1 in) along the edges of the leather template to allow for folding under.

3.

Cut the leather piece to the shape of the collar, following the chalk marking. Then snip the leather where it will fold over the collar point.

4.
Using the paintbrush, spread glue evenly over the right (outer) side of the collar.

5.
Working one side at a time, press the leather down firmly onto the collar.

6.
Turn the shirt over. Apply glue to the overhanging edges of the leather and collar and then fold onto the underside of the collar and press down firmly.

7.
Finally, use clips to secure the edge. Allow the glue to dry overnight.

SEQUIN BRA

Time: 1 hour

Skill Level: ✂ ✂ ✂

What you wear underneath your clothes is, to me, just as important as what you wear on the outside, and pretty underwear is key to feeling confident and beautiful all day long. And what could be better than when your underwear is so amazing that you want to wear sheer clothing in order to show it off? In this project, I show you how to create a simple yet eye-catching triangle bra, perfect under a vintage blouse or, for the more daring, under a semi-sheer top.

Wear It: Style this sparkly bra with a sheer T-shirt or vintage silk blouse.

Tip: Choose a sequin fabric with a matte bronze or silver sequin for a more subtle take on the sequin style.

You Will Need:

- Lightweight plain triangle bra
- 50 cm (20 in) of non-stretch sequin fabric
- Tracing paper
- Pencil
- Scissors
- Pins
- Needle and thread

How To:

1.
Lay the triangle bra on a flat surface and cover with tracing paper. Using a pencil, trace the outline of the bra where you want the sequin fabric to be (such as within the piped edge of the bra, as shown here).

2.
Cut out the triangle of tracing paper and check to make sure it fits properly on the bra.

3.

Pin the paper triangle to the sequin fabric and, using the traced triangle as a guide, cut out the sequin fabric triangle. To make the second triangle, flip the paper pattern over so it is a mirror image, and repeat the pinning and cutting.

4.

Check the triangles fit the bra and, if required, shape the fabric by cutting away any excess.

5.

Pin the sequin triangles onto the right side of the bra.

6.

Using small running stitches, secure the sequin fabric to the bra. Try to tuck the edges of the sequin fabric underneath the bra edge seam so that it looks more finished.

TWISTED TANK TOP

Time: 20 minutes

Skill Level: ✂ ✂ ✂

A simple jersey vest – or "tank" top – is one of those infinitely wearable pieces that works hard alongside other chic separates. To promote the feminine look of the humble vest, the sides are cut low to show off a layered top or decorative bra underneath. Fortunately, it's not hard to make a top like this out of a secondhand man's T-shirt. By twisting the straps of this top, you create a modern look that's light years away from the original item.

Wear It: Wear with a black lace triangle bra peeking out at the sides or over another, tigher-fitting, vest top. In a neutral hue, it makes the perfect pairing to everything from boho maxi-skirts to statement shorts.

Tip: Make sure you use a soft cotton jersey fabric as this won't need to be hemmed. The edges will just roll over naturally when washed.

You Will Need:

- Soft jersey T-shirt
- Scissors
- Sewing machine or needle and matching thread

How To:

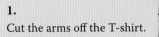

1.
Cut the arms off the T-shirt.

2.
Cut off the ribbed neckline.

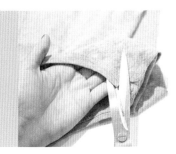

3.
Turn the vest inside out and cut along the shoulder seams, completely cutting out the seams.

4.
Twist the straps a few times (making sure to do the same number of twists on each side). The twist helps to give the top a more feminine shape.

5.
Hand or machine-stitch the two raw shoulder edges together to re-create the shoulder seam.

6.
Finally, wash on a delicate cycle. This should make the edges of the jersey roll over to give the top a more finished look.

BLANKET CAPE

Time: 2 hours

Skill Level: ✂ ✂ ✂

There's nothing more comforting in winter than wrapping yourself in a blanket and keeping toasty warm, and there's no reason why you have to be in the house in order to have this pleasure. Cocoon yourself in this cape, made from an inexpensive fleece blanket – it is one of the most stylish ways to keep warm during the colder months.

Wear It: You'll have no trouble channelling fashion-editor chic by pairing this amazing piece with a button-up blouse and cropped skinny jeans.

Tip: Choose a blanket with a tight-knit fibre, such as felt, for this project.

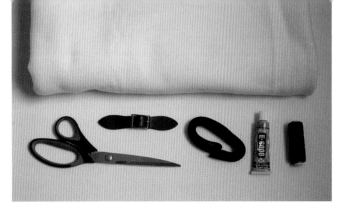

You Will Need:

- Fleece blanket measuring at least 1 m (40 in) wide by 2 m long (80 in)
- 2.5 cm (1 in) wide ribbon, 25 cm (10 in) long
- Scissors
- Needle and thread
- Industrial-strength glue, such as E6000
- Leather buckle

How To:

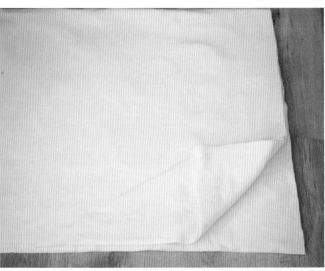

1.
Fold the blanket in half and then in half again.

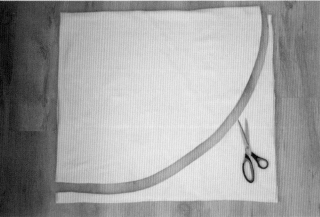

2.
Away from the folded edges, cut out a circular shape to create a rounded cape.

3.
Unfold the blanket once so it resembles a semi-circle. To create the neck opening, cut out a small semi-circle with a diameter of approximately 15 cm (6 in) through both layers of fabric in the middle of the fold.

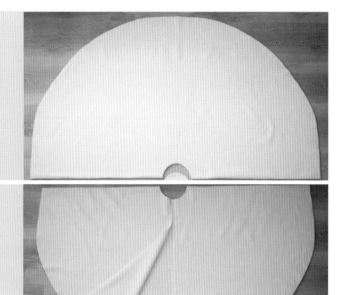

4.
To make the front opening, cut through one layer of fabric from the neck opening to the edge of the cape.

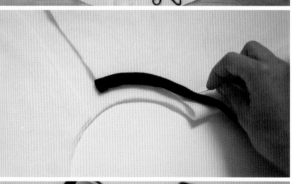

5.
Using the needle and thread, sew the ribbon to the edge of the neckline.

6.
Apply a thin layer of glue to the underside of the buckle and press onto the front of the cape.

TROUSERS & SHORTS

The foundation of a well-put-together wardrobe, trousers and shorts in classic styles can be updated to give a little more personality to your ensemble. In this section a printed fabric remnant gets turned into a pair of bang-on-trend shorts, a pair of jeans is embellished with pretty scalloped lace, and a basic pair of denim shorts is updated with a cute fabric pocket. You'll also learn how to trim a pair of shorts with lace, a technique that can be used with a multitude of different trimmings.

LACE-TRIM JEANS

Time: 30 minutes

Skill Level: ✂ ✂ ✂ ✂

Every fashionista should have a perfect pair of jeans in her wardrobe. Some of us will have a single pair that works for all occasions, while others will opt for a wardrobe brimming with different cuts, styles, colours and types of denim. Jeans are the backbone of a chic and functional wardrobe and can be worn in a multitude of ensembles to create a variety of looks.

Although classic jeans will take you everywhere, there are times when an embellished pair adds the perfect detail to an outfit. The addition of scalloped lace down the sides is just right for those occasions when you want a look that is slightly dressy but don't wish to forgo the comfort of your denims. Not only does the lace give a gorgeous detail, but it also visually elongates the legs and flatters the figure. What's more, you can add the lace for a couple of wears, then remove it when you want a change.

Wear It: Pair these lace jeans with sandals and a white T-shirt for a casual daytime look. Alternatively, combine them with a silk camisole top with suede heels for a night out with friends.

Tip: Choose lace with stretch in it for this project, so that it moves with your jeans.

Tip: Different cuts of jeans go in and out of fashion, with trends oscillating from skinnies to flares. Always choose a style that suits your body shape – this project would work perfectly with a flared style if that suits you better.

You Will Need:

- Pair of jeans
- Approximately 3 m (3¼ yd) of black lace, scalloped along one edge
- Tape measure
- Scissors
- Pins
- Needle and black thread

How To:

1.

Measure your jeans from the waist to the hem along the outer side seam. Add 10 cm (4 in) extra to the measurement so each piece of lace can be folded over by 5 cm (2 in) top and bottom and sewn to the underside of the fabric. Cut two lengths of lace to this measurement.

2.

Line up the flat edge of the lace with the side seam of the jeans and pin in place, scalloped edge facing the front of the jeans, folding over surplus at the waist and hem.

3.

Hand-stitch along the waistband to secure. Working from the waistband to the hem and along the seam edge, hand-stitch the lace to the jeans using a running stitch.

4.

Stitch to secure at the hem, then stitch along the scalloped edge in the same way. Hand-stitching works best because it allows for a little bit of stretch when you put on the jeans. Repeat on the other leg.

FLORAL SHORTS

Time: 1 hour

Skill Level: ✂ ✂ ✂ ✂ ✂

Every season, printed fabrics and patterns take centre stage in some shape or form. Whether delicate paisley prints or oversized checks, fashion designers the world over integrate them into collection after collection. This project will show you how to create a pair of chic shorts that can easily be re-created in on-trend fabrics with every season change.

Making a pair of elasticated shorts is an entry-level sewing project that's simple enough for even the most amateur sewing-machine user to try. Once embellished with lace, pom-poms or anything else you choose, these shorts take on a life of their own and integrate easily into the summer wardrobe.

The idea of working with a pattern can be daunting, so for this project you make a simple pattern from a pair of shorts you already own – there are no complicated instructions to follow or searching for your size on the pattern sheet. And because the pattern is made from something you already wear, you know it will fit you perfectly.

Wear It: Let the floral print blossom by styling this pretty pair with a simple black T-shirt and blazer.

Tip: If you have a selvedge overlocker, you should use that to finish the edges. If you don't, use a zig-zag stitch on the raw edges of the seams to reinforce and to stop fraying.

You Will Need:

- Pair of shorts to trace the pattern – I used a simple pair of denim shorts
- 2 m (2¼ yd) printed cotton fabric
- 2.5 cm (1 in) wide elastic to fit around your waist
- 1 m (40 in) craft paper
- Pen
- Ruler
- Scissors
- Thread
- Pins
- Knitting needle

How To:

1.
First make the pattern. Fold your existing shorts in half (front pockets on the outside). Lay shorts on top of craft paper and draw round them with a pen and ruler.

2.
Add 2.5 cm (1 in) to the bottom and sides of the pattern, and 4 cm (1¼ in) to the top (waistband) of the pattern. Cut out the pattern.

3.
Fold the fabric in half, wrong sides together, bearing in mind where you want your pattern to sit. Then pin the long straight edge of the pattern along the fold.

4.
Cut out the fabric along the pattern.

5.
Repeat steps 3 and 4 with the second piece of fabric so that you have two identical pieces.

6.
With right sides facing, pin the two pieces together along the two curved seams.

7.
Machine-stitch the fabric together along the two curved edges using a zig-zag stitch, following the pin line.

8.
To create the crotch, open out the shorts so that the side seams are sitting against each other. Turn under a small hem along the leg openings, then press, pin and stitch to hem the leg openings.

9.
Pin the short inside leg seams together. Using a zig-zag stitch, sew the short inner seams of the crotch.

10.
To make the elasticated waistband, follow the steps as for the Classic Maxi Skirt on pages 64–5. Finally, finish all the raw edges with a zig-zag stitch to reduce fraying and stop the shorts from splitting.

LACE-HEM SHORTS

Time: 1 hour

Skill Level: ✂ ✂

Delicate black lace-trimmed shorts, a blend of elegant and cool, are a must for every woman's wardrobe. Often this style can set you back a pretty penny, but as a DIY fashionista, why spend your hard-earned cash when you can just as easily make them yourself? With pretty eyelash lace trim and a velvet belt, this project is a stylish way to add a touch of luxury to your weekend wardrobe.

Wear It: Wear these shorts for drinks on the town with a sharp-shouldered blazer and sky-high heels.

Tip: In this project I show you how to embellish the hem of your shorts with lace, but you can also experiment with other trims, such as pom-poms, velvet, ribbons, tassels and anything else you find.

You Will Need:

- Black shorts with belt loops
- 3 m (3¼ yd) black scalloped lace
- 2.5 cm (1 in) wide black velvet ribbon measuring double the size of your waist
- Sewing machine or needle and thread
- Pins
- Scissors

How To:

1.
Measure the circumference of the leg opening and cut two lengths of lace to size, adding 5 cm (2 in) for overlapping. Pin the lace to the hem of the shorts on the right side, starting on the inside leg seam. Overlap the lace at the inner seam and trim if necessary to avoid bulk.

2.
Repeat to trim the other leg opening.

3.
Using a straight stitch on the machine or a running handstitch, sew the lace to the hem of the shorts on the right side of the fabric. Repeat for the other leg.

4.
Thread the velvet ribbon through the belt loops, cutting to size as necessary – this one is quite short but you might prefer yours with long dangling "tails".

PRINT-POCKET SHORTS

Time: 30 minutes

Skill Level: ✂ ✂ ✂

A pair of denim shorts is an absolute essential item in any warm-weather wardrobe, taking you from the beach or park and to just about everywhere else with ease. A fuss-free classic, cut-off denim shorts give weekend outfits a kick of relaxed chic. One of the simplest and most popular projects in the DIY fashionista's repertoire, it wouldn't be summer without an obligatory day spent cutting and distressing piles of jeans bought in secondhand stores.

There are so many options when it comes to embellishing denim shorts – you can choose from bleaching, studding, painting, dyeing and many, many more. This is one of my favourite options: attaching fabric pocket patches.

Wear It: Keep it simple on the beach and pair with a white T-shirt and sandals, or dress up the style for the evening with a structured blazer and the highest of heels.

Cut-off Jean Shorts

1. Put on a pair of secondhand jeans and mark how short you want to cut them.

2. Take them off and mark with tailor's chalk, measuring accurately and leaving a few inches of fabric inside the leg at the crotch. Essentially you want them to be longer on the inside seam than on the side of the leg. Cut along the marked line from the outside seam inwards.

3. Put the shorts on and check the length and style – you may want to cut a bit more off or alter them slightly. Do this patiently because there's nothing worse than cutting too much and rendering them unwearable.

4. Wash the shorts in the washing machine to get the frayed look along the hemline.

Tip: Choose any fabric you like for this project – I chose floral but you can use leopard-print, striped, polka dots – the options are endless.

You Will Need:

- Denim shorts
- Floral fabric
- Craft paper
- Scissors
- Pen
- Needle and thread

How To:

1.
Trace the outline of the pocket of the shorts onto craft paper, then cut out.

2.

Check that the pattern matches the pocket.

3.

Pin the pattern to the right side of the floral fabric and cut out, leaving 2.5 cm (1 in) all around.

4.

Use the same pattern to make a second patch.

5.

Turn under 2.5 cm (1 in), press and then pin a hem along all sides of each patch. Hand- or machine-stitch the hem to finish the edges.

6.

Pin each floral patch to each pocket and hand-stitch in place along the seam, making sure to cover the edges of the pockets.

ACCESSORIES

Usually fairly quick and easy to make, accessories can turn a classic outfit into a high-impact style statement. In this section you will learn how to create a striking studded headband, match your wristwear to your ensemble with a scarf watch, be garden-party ready with a rose headband and bring a clutch bag to life with the addition of fringing.

TASSEL EARRINGS

Time: 15 minutes, plus drying time

Skill Level: ✂

Long, shoulder-sweeping earrings make an elegant style statement and have been a fixture in my wardrobe ever since I can remember. I love their ability to instantly elevate a simple outfit, and they are perfect for going from day to night. Keep them in your handbag, along with some red lipstick, to put on in the event that you want to dress up an outfit in the evening.

Since moving to Hong Kong a few years ago, I've been overwhelmed by the number of tassels used in everyday life around the city. Although in other parts of the world you might spot them attached to curtains and in craft-supply stores, in Hong Kong they seem to be absolutely everywhere. Seeing them so much I couldn't help but become a little bit infatuated, so what better way to combine two of my favourite things than to make them into one stylish DIY project?

For this project I have chosen to use two Art Deco-style buttons to re-create a 1950s look, but you should feel free to experiment with any buttons that you have or that you like. Just make sure they have a loop on the back rather than holes through the middle so that you can secure the tassels properly.

Wear It: Pair these earrings with a strapless or bustier top to allow this statement accessory to do all the talking.

Tip: When using craft glue, always let the glue dry for a few minutes and become slightly tacky before bonding your chosen items together. This will allow it to set and hold.

You Will Need:

- 2 Art Deco-style gold buttons, with loops on the backs
- 4 small black tassels
- 2 stud earring pad-and-back sets
- Acrylic glue that dries clear

How To:

1.
Thread the ends of two of the tassels through the holes at the back of the button. Secure the tassels by tying a knot at the back.

2.
Put a small amount of glue on the back of the button above the tassels, placing according to how you want the earrings to sit on your ears.

3.
Allow the glue to become tacky, then place the earring back onto the glue and press down. Add some more glue on top if desired. Repeat for the second earring.

4.
Leave to dry overnight.

CRYSTAL RING

Time: 15 minutes, plus drying time

Skill Level: ✂

There's no denying that rings are a major style statement, with fashionistas all over the world adorning their fingers (sometimes all ten at a time) with stones, jewels and just about anything else they can find. Whether you prefer to wear one ring at a time or layer ring upon ring, there's no denying that what you wear on your fingers says a lot about your style and your look.

Beautiful crystal or stone rings can cost a fortune but the DIY-er can make her own, mixing and matching favourite looks without blowing her budget. Here, I show you how to make a simple crystal ring, a technique that can be used with any embellishment that takes your fancy, including vintage buttons.

Wear It: This high-impact accessory is perfect worn as a cocktail ring with a simple party dress.

Tip: Use heavy-duty industrial glue to ensure the stone stays attached to the ring base.

You Will Need:

- Crystal or other rock
- Ring base
- Industrial-strength glue, such as E6000

How To:

1.
Decide which side of the stone you would like the top of the ring to be.

2.
Turn the stone over and apply a grape-sized dab of glue.

3.
Wait for few moments for the glue to get tacky.
Press the ring base onto the glue.

4.
Add some more glue to the top of the ring base to ensure a strong hold. Leave overnight to dry.

DELICATE CHAIN RINGS

Time: 30 minutes

Skill Level: ✂

Delicate gold or silver jewellery rarely dates and is easy to wear with every outfit, either on its own or layered with other items. This project is a super-simple DIY that requires next to no time, few materials and a very low skill level.

Wear It: Pair these beautiful gold rings with other gold pieces or simply wear them on their own.

You Will Need:

- Beading or needlenose pliers
- Wirecutters
- 50 cm (20 in) of delicate gold chain
- Small gold jump rings (relative to the size of your chain)

How To:

1.
Take the chain and wrap it around your finger to measure how much chain you will need for the ring

2.
Using wirecutters, cut the chain to the size required for the ring.

3.
Open the jump ring using the pliers.

4.
Holding the jump ring with the pliers, put one end of the chain onto the open jump ring.

5.
Hook the other end of the chain onto the jump ring and close the jump ring using the pliers.

SCARF STRAP WATCH

Time: 30 minutes

Skill Level: ✂ ✂

When I was younger, I found it impossible to be on time. I'd never worn a watch because I'd struggled to find one that I found comfortable or that matched all my outfits, but one day an irate university lecturer, who didn't appreciate my poor time-keeping, kindly suggested I get myself a watch or find another class. Although I knew it was somewhat of a hollow threat, I realized he was right and a watch could make all the difference to my life. So I came up with this scarf strap watch where you can replace the strap of any watch with colourful fabric or a scarf.

This project allows even the most sartorially fussy woman to find something to suit her taste, and enables you to change your mind every day. You can go for a printed fabric, a block colour such as black, or even a bright pink or neon yellow.

Wear It: Match this watch to your outfit or use a bright, bold fabric for a shock of colour.

Tip: *Keep an eye out in charity shops and markets for boxes of old watches. If you're lucky you will find one that's still ticking and can use it as the basis for this project.*

Tip: *Make sure you choose a silk scarf or piece of fabric slim enough to be pulled through the strap so that it doesn't get stuck. If it does get caught, simply remove the pin and take out the fabric.*

You Will Need:

- Watch with a removable strap
- Slim silk scarf of any pattern or design
- Large straight pin
- Beading or needlenose pliers

How To:

1.
To remove the straps of your watch, use the straight pin to push out the watch pins and remove the straps.

2.
Take the pins out of the straps using the pliers.

3.
Put the pins back into their sockets and thread the scarf through them to form the straps of the watch.

4.
Pull the scarf through so that the lengths of fabric are even on each side of the watch.

5.
Wrap the scarf around your arm for some simple but seriously fun arm candy! You can tie the scarf in a big bow or wrap multiple times and secure in a small knot.

STATEMENT NECKLACE

Time: 30 minutes, plus drying time

Skill Level: ✂

A colourful necklace brings life to even the simplest outfit. The best part about this project is that practically every woman will already own at least one cheap necklace, whether it is beaded, rhinestone or plastic. Although you may think you will never have a reason to wear it again, this project will show you how it can be updated into an eye-popping piece of jewellery. I painted my necklace lilac, but you could experiment with any colour of the rainbow.

Wear It: This colour-shock style will lend a luxe edge to wardrobe favourites. For maximum impact, style it with printed trousers and a classic white T-shirt.

Tip: Always use non-toxic spray paint outdoors or in a well-ventilated area – never inside the house; spray-paint dust can settle on your furniture and be difficult to remove

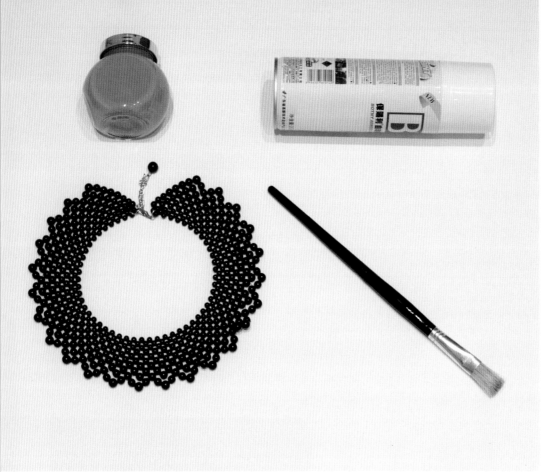

- Inexpensive beaded necklace
- White primer non-toxic spray paint
- Coloured acrylic paint
- Clear lacquer spray paint
- Craft paper or newspaper
- Paintbrush

How To:

1.
Place your necklace on craft paper or newspaper in a well-ventilated area or outdoors. Spray a couple of light, even coats, on the necklace with the white primer, allowing each coat to dry before doing the next. Avoid heavily spraying. Leave to dry overnight.

2.
Once the necklace is dry, apply several even coats of coloured acrylic paint using the paintbrush. Leave to dry overnight.

3.
Spray with clear lacquer spray paint to protect the colour from chipping.

RHINESTONE COLLAR NECKLACE

Time: 1 hour

Skill Level: ✂ ✂ ✂

Stand-alone collars are quite possibly one of the easiest accessories to make yourself, and they add a sense of fun to a classic outfit. Although collars were once the domain of school uniforms and business shirts, they are now hot fashion property.

The beauty of the collar as an accessory is that it is incredibly simple to make from a secondhand or vintage shirt and can be embellished with a multitude of craft items, such as buttons, beads and trims. Look in the men's and women's sections of your local secondhand stores for different types of collars – large, small, rounded and pointed – with which to experiment.

Wear It: Wear this chic collar necklace with a simple silk vest or over the top of a jacket or cape (such as the Blanket Cape on page 95).

Tip: *The larger the lapel, the more room you will have to embellish it with rhinestones.*

Tip: *Replace the top button on the collar with a hook and eye so the collar sits more like a necklace.*

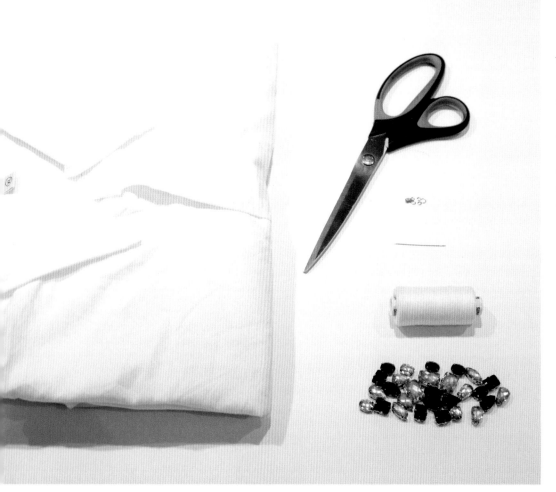

You Will Need:

- Secondhand or vintage
  white shirt
- Assorted black and white
  rhinestones in settings
- Needle and thread
- Hook and eye
- Scissors

How To:

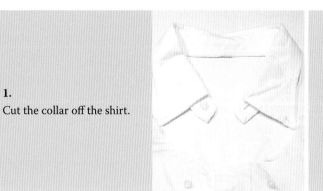

1.
Cut the collar off the shirt.

2.
Place the rhinestones
in different positions on
the lapels until you get the
design you like.

3.
Using your needle and thread, sew the rhinestones onto both lapels, making sure that the designs on each are symmetrical.

4.
Remove the top button using scissors.

5.
Sew the edges of the button and buttonhole down under the collar so they are no longer visible.

6.
Sew on the hook and eye fastening in place of the button and buttonhole.

PETER PAN COLLAR NECKLACE

Time: 20 minutes

Skill Level: ✂ ✂

This gold chain necklace is a subtle and chic take on a Peter Pan collar – that girlishly rounded slip of a collar, ever so popular with folk singers and It girls alike, that has popped up in every decade since the early 1900s: adorning adorable shift-style wedding dresses in the 1930s and '40s, as part of the mod scene of the 1960s, and on outfits of the ironically demure in the 1980s. Today designers all over the world have embraced its resurgence in popularity, creating jewellery in the Peter Pan collar style, as well as detachable collars in unexpected fabrics, such as leather.

Wear It: Pair the necklace with a simple white top and a bright collared skirt, or wear it over the top of a crisp white T-shirt or on bare skin with a strappy bustier.

You Will Need:

- Around 1 m (1 yd) of delicate gold chain
- Lobster clasp
- 5 gold jump rings
- Beading or needlenose pliers
- Scissors

How To:

1.
Cut the chain into three pieces with scissors so that one length measures around 50 cm (20 in), and the other two approximately 25 cm (10 in) long.

2.
Attach a jump ring to one end of the longer piece of chain (see page 121) and attach the lobster clasp to the other.

3.
In the very middle of the chain, attach a jump ring, then attach the two other lengths of chain to this jump ring.

4.
Put the necklace around your neck. Looking in a mirror, hold up the two loose ends of shorter chain to see where they should sit on the main part of the necklace to form the "collar". There isn't any right or wrong here – just play around until you like the shape, then attach the ends of chain to the necklace with jump rings.

ROSE HEADBAND

Time: 30 minutes

Skill Level: ✂ ✂

I'm sure you'll be wondering what to do with the fabric that will no doubt be left over from some of the projects in this book. For years this stumped me too, and I often had boxes overflowing with fabric offcuts in a rainbow of colours and fabric types. It never felt right to throw them away but I rarely found a use for them. Well, not only is this flower headband project a gorgeous addition to any summer wardrobe, it's a great way to make use of all those odd scraps in your craft box. In this version I have used red jersey cut from a skirt, but you can use any fabrics you want. Don't be afraid to mix up colours, prints and patterns. You can choose a thick linen fabric to make large flowers that stand up, or a light silk for floppy, more casual-looking flowers.

Wear It: Wear the flower headband with a cocktail dress for a garden party. For a day out shopping, team it with a relaxed outfit of jeans and a slouchy white T-shirt.

Tip: Hot glue is the best type of adhesive for this project because it is strong and dries fast, but be extra careful when using a hot glue gun, as the glue will burn you if it comes into contact with your skin.

Tip: Cut smaller circles of fabric if you want more delicate flowers.

You Will Need:

- Ready-made Alice band
- Scrap fabric
- Glue gun and glue sticks
- Scissors

How To:

1.
Cut your fabric into 20 circles, each one measuring approximately 10 cm (4 in) in diameter.

2.
Place a dab of glue into the centre of one of the fabric circles, then squeeze together to create a flower shape. Repeat to create all the "roses".

3.
Glue the flowers to the headband, one at a time, starting at one side and working towards the centre of the headband.

4.
To finish, snip the flowers to the desired size.

SPIKE HEADBAND

Time: 20 minutes, plus drying time

Skill Level: ✄

Accessories are essential to every outfit. And with a wardrobe that's filled with classic and chic pieces, they can add a sense of fun and fashion without having to splurge on a whole new outfit. The beauty of accessories is that they're relatively inexpensive. If you're on a tight budget, a few can go a long way to completely updating your outfits. And if you're a DIY enthusiast, as I am, you'll know that the best ones are those you make yourself.

Sometimes the perfect accessory involves spikes! Traditionally the domain of punks and members of biker gangs, in the past few years spikes have become incredibly popular as a way to add an eye-catching detail and an edge to an outfit. Now taking the DIY world by storm, they never fail to draw attention.

Wear It: Pair this tough accessory with a classic outfit of a black jacket, slouchy white shirt and jeans.

Tip: Choose a headband slightly wider than the width of your spikes so that they can be secured properly.

Tip: Use industrial-strength glue for this project. Most industrial glues will take a few days to set so give your hairband plenty of time to dry before heading out the door.

You Will Need:

- Ready-made Alice band measuring approximately 5 cm (2 in) wide
- 7 tree spike studs
- Industrial-strength glue, such as E6000
- Tape measure
- Tailor's chalk

How To:

1.
Measure the circumference of your headband. Mark evenly with chalk where you want the spikes to sit. I left 10 cm (4 in) at the start of the headband on each side, and a gap of 2 cm (¾ in) between each spike.

2.
Put a drop of glue on a spike and attach to the headband.

3.
Attach all the spikes in the same way.

4.
Lay the headband flat on the table to give the glue time to dry without straining the bond.

FRINGED CLUTCH

Time: 30 minutes

Skill Level: ✂ ✂

Fringing comes at the top of the list of dramatic and eye-catching embellishments in a fashionista's arsenal of style, and its texture and movement make it the perfect addition for evening accessories. Here, it turns a clutch bag into a style statement, bringing to life every outfit it accompanies.

Wear It: Team this statement piece with a classic and relaxed ensemble of pastel jeans, suede pumps and a long-line black silk blazer.

Tip: Keep your eyes peeled for extra-long fringing – the longer the fringe, the more elegant the look.

You Will Need:

- Leather or faux-leather clutch bag (one with a flap opening works best)
- Long-fringed trim
- Hot glue gun and glue
- Scissors

How To:

1.
Measure the fringe across the back of the bag and cut two pieces to fit the width.

2.
Being careful to keep the fringe in a straight line, use hot glue to attach it to the bag, approximately 5 cm (2 in) above the base of the bag.

3.
Repeat on front of the bag, ensuring that the fringe is placed at the same level as on the back of the bag; the fringe should hang to the same length back and front.

4.
If your bag has a flap, glue some fringe to the sides of the bag as well, making sure that you won't be able to see the top edge of the fringe.

PAINT-SPLATTER CLUTCH

Time: 1 hour, plus drying time

Skill Level: ✂

For me, DIY fashion projects are a way to embrace your creative side, put your own spin on an item and make something unique and individual. So there is nothing better than when projects offer all of this and are also fun to do. While some projects can be hugely involved – you can understand why it's so hard to be a fashion designer – making this project feels more like a party than an actual piece of work, and it's a great one to try out with friends.

Updating an inexpensive clutch bag using ordinary acrylic paint is an incredibly simple way of reflecting the seasons' changing colour trends without having to splurge on a new outfit. Neons, pastels, monotone – you can use just about any colour palette, provided you can find the paint.

Wear It: Team this clutch bag with a classic monotone outfit like a black full skirt and white silk shirt, emphasizing the graphic colours of your stylish new accessory.

Tip: This technique can be very messy! Work outdoors if possible.

Tip: Splatter painting is a fantastic way to update many different items in your wardrobe or things found in a secondhand store. It's very simple to do and requires few artistic skills. Just be careful not to mix the paints together once you have splattered them – unfortunately, this usually results in varying shades of brown.

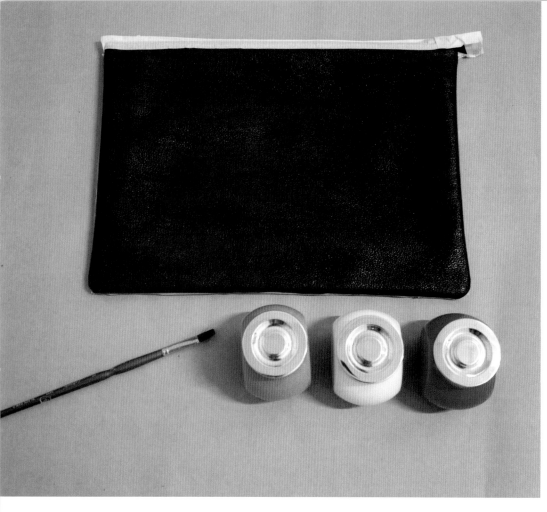

You Will Need:

- Clutch bag or oversized pencil case
- Brown paper or newspaper
- Coloured acrylic paints in red, white and lilac
- Small containers such as yogurt pots for diluting the paints
- Masking tape
- Small paintbrush
- Jar of water for rinsing the brush between colours

How To:

1.
Stick masking tape over the zip or fastening, so that paint won't get on it and render the bag unusable.

2.
Cover your painting surface with brown paper or newspaper to protect your surroundings from stray paint. Place the clutch bag on top.

3.
Water down the paints in small containers such as yogurt pots to make them more viscous but not too watery. Dip your paintbrush into the red paint, then flick it towards the bag.

4.
Wash the brush and then repeat the process with the white and lilac paint. You do not need to allow one colour to dry before applying another.

5.
Leave to dry overnight, then remove the masking tape.

SHOES

What you wear on your feet says so much about your style and the type of person that you are, and it's easy to customize your shoes using DIY to show off your individual style and sense of fashion. In this section, you'll learn how to make a chic pair of cap-toe heels, a pair of secondhand boots will be revitalized with the help of some printed fabric and you'll find out how to add a simple hint of sparkle to flat summer sandals.

PATTERNED ANKLE BOOTS

Time: 1 hour, plus drying time

Skill Level: ✂ ✂

Ankle boots are a style staple, as they go with just about everything and are so easy to integrate into an outfit. Not purely for wearing during winter, ankle boots can be paired with cut-off shorts or mini skirts during the spring and summer months. If you wear boots as much as I do, you may be wondering what to do with your favourite pair when they've seen one too many good days and nights out and are looking a little lacklustre. Instead of placing your old boots on top of the pile bound for your local secondhand store, revamp them. In this project, you will learn how to cover a pair of boots with patterned fabric, completely revitalizing them and helping you get the most out of one of your favourite wardrobe pieces.

I used a brightly patterned printed fabric, which encompassed both Aztec and floral style prints. This fabric actually come a from a dress before-and-after project I did – which goes to show you that you should always hang onto your scraps and offcuts.

Wear It: Team these boots with a tailored mini for modern appeal and match a knitted sweater to the hues of the fabric.

Tip: Want a more flattering ankle boot? Choose a style that has a "V"-shaped dip at the front, which will elongate the legs.

Tip: Use heavy-duty adhesive to ensure that your fabric sticks and doesn't fray.

Tip: When choosing fabric, go for a lightweight style so you can cut and shape it easily without damaging the shoes.

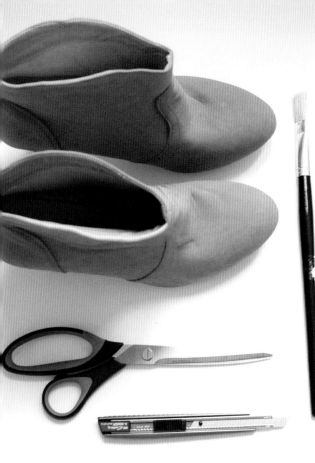

You Will Need:

- Pair of secondhand ankle boots
- Approximately 1 m (40 in) of patterned fabric
- Sewing scissors
- Heavy-duty adhesive glue
- Medium-size paintbrush
- Sponge (optional)
- Stanley knife

How To:

1.
Decide where you will be placing your fabric – for ease of shaping, chose the flattest, smoothest areas. Here I chose to cover the straight sides and top, leaving the leather heel and toe cap exposed. Measure and cut four pieces of fabric, one for each side of both shoes, ensuring the pieces are larger all round than the area you need to cover.

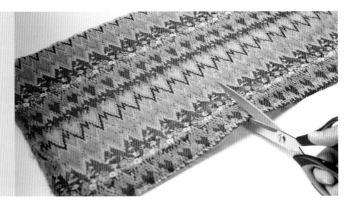

2.
Use the paintbrush to brush the glue evenly onto the area you want to cover with fabric, making sure you go all the way to the edges.

3.
Press the fabric onto one side of the shoe, smoothing down with your fingers or a sponge to remove any bubbles.

4.
Use the Stanley knife to cut the fabric to size onto the shoe, staying as close to the edges as you are able. Repeat with the other side of the shoe, overlapping the fabric slightly at the front and back joins – make sure the seam location matches the natural seam of the boot.

5.
Cut the excess fabric along the top of the boots, leaving a small allowance for turning over onto the inside of the boot.

6.
Using the paintbrush, apply glue along the inside edges of the boot. Press the fabric over the upper edges and smooth down. Leave to dry overnight.

ROSE-GOLD GLITTER SANDALS

Time: 30 minutes, plus drying time

Skill Level: ✂

Glitter is, without doubt, one of my favourite DIY materials. Although sometimes messy to work with, there is nothing quite like it for adding eye-catching sparkle to your wardrobe, be it in a simple glittery clutch bag or a full-on shimmery blazer. Glitter really gives a classic outfit a lift.

Take summer flats as the perfect example. I'm always on the look out for a pair that is comfortable enough to wear throughout the sweltering months, but also chic and stylish so that they look great with a multitude of summer outfits. Adding glitter is simple and inexpensive, and once you've completed this project, I guarantee you'll be looking in your closet wondering what else you can cover!

Before you begin, consider what colour glitter would flatter and work best with your wardrobe. For this project, I mixed gold and silver to create a rose-gold colour, which is much less brassy than gold on its own.

Wear It: These glittery sandals look great when paired with denim shorts and a Breton top during summer.

Tip: *For a professional-looking finish, use masking tape to cover the areas where you don't want any glitter.*

Tip: *Wherever possible, work with glitter outside or in the bathroom, so you can contain any spills and wipe all surfaces clean after you have finished the project.*

You Will Need:

- Thick-strap sandals
- Masking tape
- Coloured glitter (I chose gold and silver)
- Small plastic container
- Acrylic glue
- Small, flat paintbrush
- Plastic container for mixing the glitter
- Clear gloss spray

How To:

1.
Cover the base of the front of both sandals with masking tape, turning under at all edges.

2.
Pour the glitter into the container – I chose to make a rose-gold shade by mixing two-thirds gold to one-third silver glitter, gently shaking the colours together to combine.

3.

Add a little glue to the glitter, then mix together. Add enough glue to create a thick, cement-like consistency.

4.

Using the paintbrush, spread the mixture on the front strap of both shoes.

5.

Sprinkle a little extra dry glitter over the straps to ensure they are well coated. Leave to dry, then shake to remove any excess glitter. Finally, spray the front of the sandals with gloss spray to seal in the glitter, and then remove the masking tape.

SPIKE HEELS

Time: 30 minutes

Skill Level: ✂ ✂

Classic shoes, like a pair of high heels, are investment pieces and are sure to get a workout in any fashionista's wardrobe. Every woman should have a pair of heels that turns a casual outfit into something amazing and makes her feel like a million dollars. Here I have updated a pair of red suede high courts with some tough-looking spikes – perfect as a dramatic statement shoe.

Wear It: Pair these heels with a simple outfit of skinny jeans and a black jacket for a look that's all about the shoes.

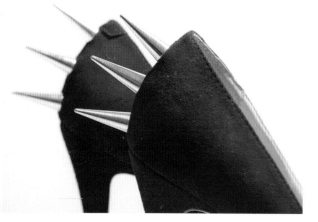

Tip: Spikes are very simple to use when you have the right tools. It's worth investing in a dart awl (a tool for making holes in leather and fabric) if you plan on doing any heavy-duty studding or spiking projects.

You Will Need:

- Leather or suede high heels
- Soft pencil
- Dart awl
- 6 cone spikes and matching screws
- Screwdriver

How To:

1.
On the inside seam of each shoe, mark the position of three spikes with the pencil – the spikes shouldn't be too close to each other, to make it less of a strain on the seam. At each of the pencil marks, push the awl through the seam from the inside of the shoe and wiggle it to create a hole.

2.
Push a screw through one of the holes from inside the shoe, using a screwdriver to twist it through if this proves difficult to do.

3.
Twist a spike onto the screw, then use a screwdriver to secure it tightly in place. Make sure the screws are flush with the leather on the inside so they won't rub the backs of your heels. Repeat for the remaining spikes.

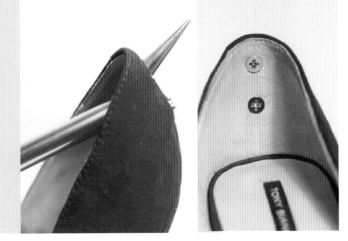

CAP-TOE HIGH HEELS

Time: 1 hour, plus drying time

Skill Level: ✂ ✂

What you wear on your feet says a lot about who you are, and interesting footwear never fails to catch my eye and make me wonder about the wearer. The cap-toe has an elegance that works perfectly in a classic wardrobe, surely due in part to the two-tone cap shoes Coco Chanel made so popular in the 1950s. This version takes the colour blocking further with caps on both the toes and the heels. You can be as creative as you like with the shades: black goes with everything, but you could also experiment with coloured or even white caps.

Wear It: I love to wear these shoes with a tonal outfit of pink and black or, when I want to let the shoes stand out, a classic black and white outfit.

Tip: *If you are concerned that the paint may crack when you remove the tape, leaving you with an unattractive serrated edge, remove the tape while the paint is still slightly tacky, as it will be more likely to leave a clean line.*

Tip: *Spray leather shoes with a coat of clear lacquer once the paint is dry in order to protect the cap-toes from scuff marks. It will also help keep the leather looking new. However, avoid using lacquer on fabric shoes, like the pink heels used here, as it may cause the fabric to discolour.*

You Will Need:

- Brightly coloured pointed high heels
- Black acrylic paint
- Masking tape
- Small, flat paintbrush

How To:

1.
Carefully mask off the area that you don't want to paint at the front of both shoes, making sure that they are identical. Press the tape down firmly.

2.
Do the same for the back of both shoes, again making sure that the areas to be painted are identical.

3.
Paint the toe of the shoes with black acrylic paint in a thin coat. Repeat until the colour underneath is completely covered, allowing each coat to dry before applying the next.

4.
Paint the back of the shoes and the heels with the black acrylic paint in the same way as the toes. Leave to dry overnight.

5.
Remove the masking tape carefully.

FRINGED ANKLETS

Time: 15 minutes

Skill Level: ✂ ✂

Every season, without fail, at least one designer makes humble suede fringing the focus of their collection. Boho, Western, Aztec – designers absolutely love fringing and always seem to be able to integrate it in some way. The suede variety is also adored by fashionistas all over the world because it's such an effective embellishment.

In this project, you will learn how to make detachable fringed anklets. Although accessorizing your accessories may seem strange, you will be able to wear these anklets with just about any pair of shoes, or wear the same classic shoes time and time again but altering the look with a different colour or type of fringing. These anklets are a true case of making your wardrobe work for you and not the other way around!

Wear It: Wear these suede anklets over the top of black flat sandals for a casual look, or with black strappy heels for a party feel.

Tip: *The technique of wrapping these anklets to create the layered fringe means that this is an incredibly simple and effective project – you'll be out the door in your favourite black heels in no time!*

You Will Need:

- 1 m (1 yd) black suede
  (or faux suede) fringed trim
- 6 jump rings
- 2 small lobster clasps
- 10 cm (4 in) of gold chain
- Beading or needlenose pliers
- Scissors
- Pins

How To:

1.
Cut the trim in half, then make a hole with the pin through one end of the first piece of trim.

2.
Thread a jump ring through the hole, leaving the ring open.

3.
Cut the chain in half with the scissors.

4.
Attach one length of chain to the jump ring and squeeze the ring with the pliers to close tightly. Add another jump ring to the other end of the chain.

5.
Make a hole with the pin in the other end of the trim, and thread through another jump ring. Attach one of the lobster clasps to the jump ring and then close it off with the pliers. Repeat for the other length of fringing.

6.
To wear, simply wrap the fringes around your ankles over a favourite pair of black heels and use the lobster clasps to hold them in place.

WARDROBE REHAB:
6 STEPS TO WARDROBE PERFECTION

- Do you ever find yourself staring into your crowded closet thinking, "I've got nothing to wear?"
- Does it take you an eternity to pick out an outfit?
- Do you feel like lots of your clothes don't suit your style or taste?
- Do you always feel like an outfit would be perfect if only you had that one key item?

If you answered yes to any of the questions above, you probably need to revitalize your wardrobe, not purely through shopping but by critically evaluating what you have and making a plan for your aspirations. The good news is that the basis for this fantastic new wardrobe is lurking in the depths of your current wardrobe – all you need to do is rehabilitate it. Why buy when you can DIY? Follow these simple steps to be well on your way to a functional and chic wardrobe with endless outfit options.

STEP 1: SPRING CLEAN

STEP 2: DEFINE YOUR STYLE

STEP 3: WARDROBE ESSENTIALS

STEP 4: COLOURS

STEP 5: STAY ORGANIZED

STEP 6: FOCUS YOUR SHOPPING

STEP 1: SPRING CLEAN

A crowded wardrobe is never conducive to quick, easy and chic dressing and therefore the most important step on the path to a highly functional wardrobe is culling it to a manageable size, with only things in it that look good on you, are in good condition and which you actually wear.

The Sorting-by-Piles Method

1   Sort your clothes by type (tops, jackets, dresses, skirts, short and trousers) and then get to work trying everything on. Every single thing.

2   Make five different piles of clothes: one for clothes to keep, one for clothes to sell, one for clothes to give away, one for clothes for DIY projects and a final one for clothes that need altering or mending in order to become wearable.

3   When trying on the clothes in front of a long mirror, ask yourself:
- "When was the last time I wore this?" If you haven't worn the item in the last 12 months (taking into account the season), you probably aren't going wear it again.
- "Does this make me feel attractive?" If you look at yourself in the mirror and what you're trying on doesn't make you feel your best (wrong shape, colour or style), think about getting rid of it. If it doesn't make you feel good, you'll be much less likely to wear it.
- "Does this fit properly?" Check the fit by lifting your arms, sitting down, bending over, etc. Eliminate anything that is too big or too small.
- "Is this item out of date?" Some fashions and prints will date quickly and if you haven't worn it because it reflects a trend that has passed completely, you'll not wear it again soon.
- "Is this item worn out?" If the item isn't in good condition and is ripped, stained or stretched, don't hang onto it unless you are committed to fixing the problem.

- "Does this need altering?" If something doesn't sit or fit quite right but is well made and of good quality, see if you can get it altered professionally or alter it yourself.

4   Repeat steps 1 to 3 above for shoes, accessories and underwear. Anything you haven't worn or used in a while or is in bad condition needs to go.

Once you have done all of this, you should have one pile of items that look and feel great. This is the basis from which you will develop a gorgeous and satisifying wardrobe.

What About the Other Piles?
- **Sell:** For items that are of high quality and good condition, sell them on eBay, to your friends through Facebook, take them to a clothes swap or sell them at a market or car-boot or garage sale.
- **Give Away:** For clothes that are not worth investing your time in selling, bag them up and take them to your local charity or secondhand shop, or give them to a friend or your relatives.
- **DIY:** Keep a few items to experiment with, but make sure you have some idea of what you're going to do with them and make time to do it, otherwise they'll just sit around collecting dust forever.
- **Alter or Mend:** For those things that need a bit of tweaking to work perfectly, make time to get them to a dressmaker or modify them yourself. If they don't fulfil the criteria above once altered, add them to the selling or giving-away pile.

Although it's difficult to get rid of clothes you like, if they are not currently being worn, it's best to remove them from cluttering up your wardrobe. You can always give them to a friend or sibling if they are expensive – or put them in a box marked "to give to my daughter one day". Don't we all wish our mother had kept those amazing outfits she wore 30 years ago?

STEP 2: DEFINE YOUR STYLE

Defining your style is a very important step towards ensuring that your wardrobe works well, looks gorgeous and is also functional. Defining your style is about deciding what looks good and suits you, and then weaving in trends and experimenting with looks from there.

Assess the "Good" Pile

Remember the pile of "keepers" from when you spring-cleaned your wardrobe? Well, hopefully this pile says something about how you like to dress and what your style is. These are the clothes that you obviously enjoy wearing and (should) look good on you. Ask yourself:

"What are their characteristics?"

"What do I like about them?"

"What principles of this pile can I apply to my future shopping so that everything in my wardrobe is enjoyable to wear?"

You don't necessarily have to let this pile define you, and maybe you want to break out of your current style and start dressing differently, but understanding completely what is in your wardrobe in terms of styles and cuts is key.

Know What Suits You

Knowing your body shape and what looks good on you is important when it comes to defining your personal style. We are constantly bombarded with new trends and looks, and not everything we see will suit us and work with our body shape. Buying into every new trend and filling our wardrobes with unsuitable items is never a good idea. When in doubt about your style, choose your best features and make sure the items in your wardrobe are promoting them.

Get Inspiration

Look to magazines or online for style inspirations and start making a file of images of things you like. Stick with classic styles if you have trouble narrowing down what you like.

STEP 3: WARDROBE ESSENTIALS

Choosing your essential pieces is the starting point to any good outfit. There's no set list of a "capsule wardrobe", as it will come down to personal taste, your body, your style and a whole host of other things. What you can do, though, is determine your own list based on what you love wearing and what looks good on you. For example, this might include a classic trench and a well-cut black blazer, a maxi skirt, a little black dress, the perfect pair of jeans, Breton tops and simple silk camis, plus accessories.

STEP 4: COLOURS

The colours in your wardrobe will be a key factor in how easily you can pair items together and how functional your wardrobe is. When buying basic pieces and essentials, stick to a neutral palette of black, navy, beige or white (or any other colour you wear a lot and think of as part of your "base" outfit palette).

Add "Pops" of Colour

Once you have a smaller, manageable wardrobe with lots of well-fitting neutral essentials, purchase a few coloured items (from the high street or charity shops) each season to mix with your basics and make them more on trend.

Tip: Dress for you. Choosing colours that suit your look and skin tone is much more important than strictly adhering to trends. The season might be pushing washed-out blue but if it doesn't suit you, don't be tempted.

STEP 5: STAY ORGANIZED

There are many options when deciding how to organize your closet, but keep in mind that the overall purpose is to make it easy for you to get dressed and look great. If you have a big enough collection of clothes and a wardrobe with different compartments, sort your clothes into types (trousers, shorts/skirts, jackets, tops, shirts) and then organize by colour within their types. If you have enough room, try to hang as much as possible up. Drawers are great for jeans and underwear but you are much more likely to pull something off the rack than out of a bottom drawer. If possible store accessories and shoes at eye level and jewellery on a hanging rack.

STEP 6: FOCUS YOUR SHOPPING

The final step is to put a few rules in place to focus your future shopping, so you don't end up with a disorganized wardrobe again or buy things you won't wear and don't need. Here are some shopping rules to keep you focused.

1. Stick to a list: When you collate your list of essentials (step 3), there are probably a few things that are on the list but you don't own. If there are things that you truly need that will make your whole wardrobe more wearable – a navy blazer or well-cut pair of black trousers, for example – put these items on the list and save up to buy the best quality you can afford. Go without anything else and keep that item in mind while you are saving.

2. Don't go to sales unless you have a specific item in mind. How many times have you nipped out to have a quick look in the sales and come back with something that will only be worn a couple of times. All this does is add to the clutter in your life. Add up all the stray small bits of cash you spend this way in a year, and that is a lot of money that could buy something of good quality and infinitely wearable.

3. Limit the amount of cheap clothing you buy. When you can, head to charity shops. Often you find better quality garments in secondhand and vintage stores than you do in high-street chainstores.

RESOURCES & SUPPLIERS

Resources

Online Inspiration Sources

Looking for ideas for your next DIY project?
These are the places I often look online for my inspiration.

Glitter Guide

http://theglitterguide.com

A treasure trove of glittery home and fashion inspiration.

Jak&Jil

http://jakandjil.com

The master of detailed street style imagery – Tommy Ton's photos are more often than not filled with runway-ready DIY inspiration for you to start working on.

Martha Stewart

www.marthastewart.com

Learn the basics of DIY with the veteran of craft and home improvement.

Net-a-porter

www.net-a-porter.com

My go-to place for online window shopping, I spend hours here looking at products to inspire my next project.

Pinterest

http://pinterest.com

The perfect place to find and store your DIY inspiration.

Refinery 29

www.refinery29.com

One of my favourite fashion news sites – they often do their own DIY projects with techniques that help to inspire me.

Style.com

www.style.com

My go-to for runway DIY inspiration, including imagery of every collection. The detailed shots of runway shows is incredibly useful DIYers busy working out how to make their clothes.

Vanessa Jackman

http://vanessajackman.blogspot.com

Another amazing streetstyle website, this time with a focus on real women decked out in chic ensembles that inspire infinitely wearable DIY projects and wardrobe choices.

Vogue.com

www.vogue.com

Another runway fashion site, I often head here to keep on top of trends and collections so I know what I will be making next.

Who What Wear

www.whowhatwear.com

This style site hits the nail on the head with trend reports and is an essential source for future project ideas.

DIY Fashion Bloggers

There are many amazing bloggers out there who do DIY projects which will no doubt influence you. Below I've listed a few of the ones that inspire me on a daily basis.

Because I'm Addicted

http://becauseimaddicted.net

Geri posts daily fashion inspirations as well as on-trend projects that usually take no more than a few steps.

Honestly WTF

http://honestlywtf.com

Erica and Lauren never fail to inspire me with their simple DIY projects.

I Spy DIY

www.ispydiy.com

On her blog, as well as in her book, Jenni creates amazing DIY projects that make catwalk-ready fashion accessible to all.

Love Aesthetics

http://love-aesthetics.blogspot.com

Ivania's innovative projects are always simple and true to her unique sense of style.

Love Maegan

www.lovemaegan.com

A treasure trove of DIY fashion and home projects.

Park and Cube

www.parkandcube.com

Shini's blog is a beautifully curated collection of images of her life and style – with lots of amazing and perfectly executed DIY projects thrown in for good measure.

PS I Made this

http://psimadethis.com

One of my first DIY inspirations, Erica creates simple projects inspired by of-the-minute trends.

Sewing

Burdastyle.com

www.burdastyle.com

Pattern making tips and a valuable resource for anything sewing related.

DIY Couture

www.diy-couture.co.uk

Rosie shows you how to create your own garments from scratch without using a pattern.

Youtube

www.youtube.com

For step by step sewing techniques, head over to youtube where you will often find videos that will show you exactly what to do.

Buying for DIYing

Finding the components for your projects is a major factor in re-creating the perfect catwalk look. In addition to the information provided in the Materials section of this book (see pages 10–5), I have here listed particular brands and stores that are my regular shopping haunts.

For Basics

American Apparel

www.americanapparel.net

This store is great for on-trend premium basics that can be updated.

ASOS

www.asos.com

A mega online retailer, ASOS stocks an incredibly affordable own-brand that can be used to experiment with DIY projects.

H & M

www.hm.com

Many of the projects in this book were done using basic pieces from H&M that are perfect for simple or more complex updates.

K Mart

www.kmart.com

Another go-to store for inexpensive home and fashion items that can be used for your projects – look out for rugs to make the bodycon rug dress.

Target

www.target.com

Good for finding basics for home projects.

For Glues
3M

www.3m.com

3M is a resource for dependable glues and industrial adhesives, where you'll find products for a multitude of projects. You'll also find a huge range of other items that can be used in your projects, such as office supplies.

Beacon 527

www.beaconadhesives.com

Fast-drying, industrial strength and clear drying, this glue is flexible and waterproof when dry. It takes about 2 hours to dry and 24 hours to fully cure.

E6000

A gel glue that is perfect for use in a huge range of projects – this glue has the strength of epoxy formulas without the need to mix two ingredients.

Elmer's

www.elmers.com

Elmers has a huge range of craft glues, I use their simple white PVA glue for a large number of my projects.

Gem Tac Glue

www.beaconadhesives.com

A nontoxic water-based glue that is washable after 24 hours, this is a popular choice for securing gemstones and crystals to fabric.

G-S Hypo Cement

http://gshypocement.com

With a very fine nozzle for detailed work, this medium-strength cement takes 10–15 minutes to dry and becomes fully set in an hour. Useful for bonding nonporous surfaces such as jewellery, plastics, metals and ceramics, there is also a Fabric Cement version for textiles, leather, paper and yarn.

Krazy Glue

www.krazyglue.com

A great source for super glues.

For Sewing Machines
Singer

www.singer.com

I swear by my Singer sewing machine, and their website is a fantastic resource for sewing tips and tricks as well on advice about purchasing your first machine.

For Craft Needs

Clorox
www.clorox.com
My go-to for tie-dying and dip-dying with bleach.

Dylon
www.dylon.co.uk
All you need to know about dyeing, including a huge range
of machine and hand-washable colours.

John Lewis
www.johnlewis.com
Great resource for fabrics, sewing machines and haberdashery,
as well as all kinds of craft products, in the UK.

Michaels
www.michaels.com
A mecca for all your craft needs in the United States, go online
or visit your local store.

Rit Dye
www.ritdye.com
For all your dyeing project needs – check out their website
for interesting project ideas.

Scotch
www.scotchbrand.com
Tapes and adhesive supplies of all types including duct
and painter's tapes.

Sharpie
ww.sharpie.com
Permanent pens for craft, including fabric markers and
a huge range of other pen products.

Swarovski Crystals
www.swarovski.com
Amazing for adding a sparkle to your next project – and few
Swarovski crystal beads go a long way.

Hardware

B&Q
www.diy.com
A major hardware outlet in the UK where you will find everything
from paints to tools.

Bunnings
www.bunnings.com.au
Australia's biggest hardware outlet.

Home Depot
www.homedepot.com
Hardware store based in the USA, you will find all you need
for DIY projects, from tools to adhesives to hardware.

Local Hardware Stores
Don't forget to check out your locally owned hardware stores;
most towns and cities will have a few independently run shops.

INDEX

ACKNOWLEDGEMENTS

Author's Acknowledgements

First and foremost I want to thank the readers of my blog – your kind words and loyalty is what has driven me to continuously do bigger and better projects, and your advice when things could be done better has helped me improve everyday. Without you this book would be just a dream, and I want to thank you from the bottom of my heart.

To Ben, without your keen design eye, practical mind and unwavering patience this book could and would never have happened. You've helped me every step of the way and I can't thank you enough. I couldn't think of a better person to work with and I can't wait to see what we get up to next.

To my mum, thank you for supporting every one of my ideas (ridiculous or otherwise) and teaching me way back before they were cool that secondhand stores are the place to start when hunting for a new outfit. Your non-conformist approach to fashion and belief in "making do" forced me to look creatively at what was available me – a skill that I will take with me everywhere I go.

To my dad, the original inventor, your penchant for tinkering away at projects and finding design solutions where most would see none has become the story of my life. I wouldn't be me if it wasn't for you.

To my brother, who spent the first half of his life being prodded for reviews on my nightly fashion parades through the house, thank you for always believing in me.

To my friends and family who taught me all I know and never blinked an eye at my hand-made ensembles, even in my teens when there was always a potential wardrobe malfunction around the corner and a trail of glitter everywhere I went. Thanks to one friend in particular who remarked many moons ago that I should blog about my DIY projects – it's amazing to think that this one comment caused a domino affect that has culminated in a book and a career in what I love to do the most – make and create the things I wear, and share that with others.

To my editor Lisa, thank you for your faith in my abilities from the start and for helping me be true to myself in this book.

And finally, thank you to the amazing community of bloggers out there who inspire me daily, I feel so lucky to be part of such a kind and sharing group of people and I can't help but feel we are helping to dramatically change the way the world consumes and enjoys fashion.

Picture Credits

thinkstockphotos.co.uk: 8, /istockphoto: 18t, 20, / Zoonar: 18b

Getty Images: /Matthew Ward: 162